# *Of* WOMB *and* TOMB

Prayer *in* Time *of* Infertility, Miscarriage, *and* Stillbirth

EDITED BY
KATE WILLIAMS

GIA PUBLICATIONS, INC.
CHICAGO

The editor wishes to acknowledge the assitance of David Philippart in selecting the prayers for this resource, and for his contribution to the section "How to Use This Book."

G-9816

Copyright © 2019 GIA Publications, Inc.
7404 S. Mason Ave., Chicago, IL 60638
www.giamusic.com

ISBN: 978-1-62277-363-3

Cover and layout design by Andrew Schultz

# CONTENTS

# FOREWORD

The book of Ecclesiastes tells us that there is a season for everything: a time to be born, and a time to die; a time to weep, and a time to laugh; a time to mourn, and a time to dance. We eagerly welcome the opportunities to laugh and dance, but outside the regular parish funeral, we can struggle to make equal room in our communities for openly acknowledging the times for weeping, for mourning, for dying.

Those who struggle with the inability to conceive, those who know the pain of losing a child before birth, and those who have faced their infant's death at the time of birth know that this season of mourning is often held inside, hidden and unseen. What was anticipated to be a joyful and exciting time becomes, instead, a plunge into despair. Couples expecting to announce to the world a sign of their love in a visible, living, co-creation with God are instead met with feelings of confusion, disappointment, fear, and anxiety. Women who spend their whole lives dreaming of their role in bearing light to the world in the form of a child now shift to dark questions about their own value and worthiness; their bodies, once a source of life, have become in this moment a place of death. Some have redefined their lives after their experience. Some look for solace over and over again, as each encounter with loss permanently weaves itself into their story. For many, marriages become strained, the weight of doubt and grief is isolating, and even the conversation with God seems quiet.

But God does not abandon us. Somehow, on the other side of loss an incredible story of resilience emerges. Bodies, though they are never the same again, heal. Couples try again, adopt, or reimagine. Those who mourn in isolation find not one, not two, but a community of others with whom they can identify. God's silence is not absence; it is the patient listening of a God who knows our grief first-hand, who weeps with us, who holds us as a mother holds her child. Death is never the whole story. The hope of new life surprises, confounds, persists.

We can do better in our parish ministries to acknowledge this kind of loss, and to be open to the seemingly impossible ways in which God puts life in the places where we knew only death. If the statistics are accurate—about ten percent of couples struggle to conceive, and one out of four pregnancies ends in loss—then we simply must do better to serve the significant number of people of our communities who carry this type of grief, whether it be decades old or new and raw.

The goal of this resource is to be of service to individuals, couples, and parish communities who wish to accompany those on their grief journey. The prayers, poems, and stories found in this book may provide comfort when read alone or with a spouse, or as a guide in creating prayer opportunities for the community at large. The companion recording (CD-1061) may be used in private prayer or as a demonstration tool for preparing music for parish prayer. The printed music collection (G-9817), which corresponds to the selections found on the recording, offers some ideas for congregational use but certainly does not exhaust the possibilities. Those planning prayer services should pay special attention to the particular needs of the community, taking care to not overburden or distract the participants with an abundance of new music or words. The templates for rituals in this book provide an example of what might be offered, but they should always be modified to the particular circumstances they wish to serve. Though many of the prayers and rites referenced in this book are from the Roman Catholic tradition, slight adaptations are encouraged if this would make them more appropriate for ecumenical use.

The resulting compilation is far from complete. Though we might dream of making a comprehensive resource for grieving this kind of pain, there is no single experience of grief or loss. It is my hope that the pages to come may provide a good starting place for those who wish to bring comfort and consolation. Notably absent from the enclosed material are prayers, poems, and songs in languages other than English. In particular, in light of the large and ever-growing Spanish-speaking community in the United States, it is my hope that there will soon be an edition of this book or a companion resource that more adequately represents the face of our local church. Until then, it is imperative to consider the needs and customs of the local worshiping community, creating a solution that best serves the needs of those who will pray these prayers.

It was my own familiarity with some of the pain and loss this collection seeks to address that led to my passion for bringing this resource to the world. I have been deeply changed by the willingness of so many who have had the courage and risked their vulnerability to voice their concerns, share their journeys, and advocate for themselves and for others who look to the Church to be the place we can turn to for healing and comfort. My own fears of entering into this conversation have been turned into hope that surpasses understanding, instilling a sense of responsibility to this sacred opportunity to reach out and touch the wounds of the living body. As this resource grows and develops over time, I invite you to reach out and share your experiences, so that as one Body we may all continue to heal and grow.

May we learn to be ever more present to and grateful for the Risen One among us, the God who remains with us through all seasons of life, who hears our cries, lifts us from our graves, and turns our mourning into dancing. Together, let us bear witness to the Christian mystery—that new life is born of the womb and the tomb.

—Kate Williams
February 2, 2019
The Feast of the Presentation of the Lord

# How *to* Use This Book

**Sacred Stories**

From five different individuals come five different experiences of grief. Though these examples do not exhaust the myriad perspectives of loss, they provide a sense of identity and belonging to those who relate to the feelings articulated. Pastors, pastoral associates, sacramental or grief ministers, liturgists, music directors, friends, and family members are invited to use these accounts to consider possible ways that grief works in and through the lives of those it touches. If you have experienced infertility, miscarriage, or stillbirth, perhaps you will find resonance in these reflections. No two experiences of suffering and grief are the same, but there is opportunity for peace and healing in hearing the stories of others, and in being able to tell our own.

**Poems, Hymns, and Blessings**

Filled with imagery that captivates and comforts, this section aims to put our deepest prayers into lyrical language. Through the beauty of metaphor and rhythm, we are called to both pay attention and look beyond; this invitation accompanies us throughout the stages of grief. Individuals might find hope in the ability of these texts to articulate the paradox of joy and pain. Ministers may find many passages will assist in preparing prayer. In particular, the hymn texts may be set to music for use in liturgies or prayer services. Some hymn tunes and published musical settings are suggested beneath selected texts.

## Prayers for the Child *and* Prayers of/for the Parents and Those Who Mourn

Drawing from the wisdom of several faith traditions, these sections present a number of prayers for the child and for all who mourn. Though they were initially designed for communal use, you may find the comfort of God's presence when reading these prayers alone, or sharing them with a spouse, partner, or family member.

## Scriptures

God is present in the holy Scriptures, and it is Christ himself who speaks when the Word of God is proclaimed in the gathered assembly. The selected portions of Scripture were chosen to accompany, comfort, and even challenge us in our deepest grief.

If you are experiencing infertility, miscarriage, or stillbirth, return to this section often. You could skim the various passages, returning to one that piques your interest. Or you could begin with the first passage—Jesus inviting the children to come to him—and read through the passages one a day, one a week, or in whatever way is helpful.

Don't worry about analyzing the Scripture or trying to understand all of its layers of meaning. That's good to do another time. If a question about meaning becomes persistent, jot it down and ask someone who might be able to answer it later. Now, allow the words to wash over you and cover you like a blanket. Know that God is embracing you. Read the passage slowly, perhaps even aloud. Notice what word, phrase, or image jumps out at you. When you have read the entire Scripture, rest for a moment in God's presence. Repeat over and over again the word, phrase, or image. Rest again for a moment. Then read the entire passage again. Repeat this process as much as will be helpful.

If you are preparing a group prayer, rite, or liturgy (other than evening or morning prayer), begin by choosing a passage from one of the four gospels: Matthew, Mark, Luke, or John. Then think about the people who will assemble. How much Scripture will this group benefit from hearing? If the assembly will include many small children, for example, one reading from the gospel may be sufficient. For an assembly of people who don't regularly participate in prayer or liturgy, a gospel passage alone, or perhaps paired with one other reading from outside the gospels, might be best. For an assembly of people who often participate in Sunday Mass, the Sunday Mass pattern might be best: a first reading from the First (Old) Testament, a psalm, a second reading from the Second (New) Testament, a reading from one of the four gospels.

Evening prayer and morning prayer each have only one Scripture reading, which can be from the First (Old) or Second (New) Testament, but not from the psalms or gospels. This is because the psalms are sung, and the gospel "reading" is the singing of the Canticle of Mary (evening) or the Canticle of Zechariah (morning)—both of which are gospel passages from Luke.

Be sure that each reader is given the passage as soon as possible, urging them to practice reading it aloud before the people gather.

**Psalmody**

The psalms are the ancient songs of God's People, Israel; they are sung, too, by the Church. The emotions they convey are raw, and nourish an intimacy with God. The selection of psalms here can give voice to feelings and fears in this time of grief.

When prayed in a liturgy, or with a large assembly of people, it is preferable for the psalms to be sung. Parish music ministers can help find musical settings, some of which may already sound familiar to the worshiping community.

When prayed in smaller groups, if singing is not possible, one person can lead with all repeating the verse listed as the "response." A leader says the response and all repeat it. Then the leader or leaders read each verse, with all saying the response at the end of the verse, as the *R/.* indicates.

The psalms may also be prayed in solitude, with or without repeating the response.


## Rites and Rituals

God has given us the gift of ritual as a privileged way of entering into and dwelling in the divine presence. God is indeed present to us always and everywhere. But our human capacity to be aware of God's presence is often limited. Ritual, when done well, helps us transcend our limits in sensing God's presence, responding to it in ways faithful to our covenant with God. Ritual also builds and strengthens community. A community embracing us in love and support is the most profound of God's responses to one's deepest grief upon suffering a loss. And the most profound experience of that community is revealed in its gathering to enact rituals and raise a unified cry of lament and hope in prayer.

You may wish to have a funeral for the child, in which case, your local parish can guide you through the preparation. The *Order of Christian Funerals* provides many helpful Scripture readings and prayers for the funeral of a child, baptized or unbaptized.

The Rites and Rituals section includes five orders of service, each fulfilling a specific need or circumstance, but all of which offer a tone of grace and peace. These may be used in addition to (or instead of) a funeral. None of the five services require an ordained minister to preside. Each does, however, require proper preparation.

Each of these rituals needs different kinds of leaders: a presider, a leader of singing, and one or more readers of Scripture. Be sure to provide the parts of the service to all leaders as soon as possible before the ritual, in order to foster comfort and familiarity with their assigned roles. It's important that each leader also knows the big picture, too—what comes when.

If you are experiencing or have experienced the death of a child before or at birth, contact your pastor, parish priest, liturgy director, music director, pastoral associate, minister of care, or bereavement minister for help, especially if you would like to hold such a rite in the church building. But any of these services can be held at home, too.

Day and Time

Choose a day and time that make it possible for all to gather. Be sure people know they are invited, and how important it is that they come. These rites may be celebrated whenever the family is ready: immediately after the child's death, many weeks or months later, even years later.

The "Prayer with Siblings, Cousins, and Other Children" may be most beneficial when used close to the time those children are informed of the loss. As the name might suggest, the "Evening Liturgy of the Word and Ritual of Light" contains a candle-lighting ritual that works best when it is dark outside. The other rites work at any time of day.

Setting Up a Good Place

Whether in church or at home, set up the place to best serve the ritual and those coming to participate. After estimating the number of people expected, provide a place for each, a song sheet or book (when needed) for each, and anything else the ritual may require (e.g., a candle for each if using the "Evening Liturgy of the Word and Ritual of Light").

When possible, arrange for seating that allows the members of the assembly to see each other's faces, as well as the faces of the presider, leader of singing, and reader of Scripture. The face of each person who comes is an icon, a sacred image, of the loving God who gathers us together.

Carefully read through the rite far enough ahead of time in order to gather all the accoutrements that the rite requires. This varies by rite. If incense is to be used at home, be aware of smoke detectors.

Two colors that traditionally speak of sorrow and hope in eternal life are violet and white. Lit candles, vases of flowers, plants, carefully draped fabrics—all help create a suitable place for ritual prayer. It's best to use *real* things, candles that are lit with flame (not battery-powered), fresh-cut flowers, living plants—these speak most clearly about the goodness of God.

Singing and a Leader of Singing Are Essential

Singing is absolutely integral to a ritual's power and effectiveness. And while listening to someone sing, whether live or via recording, can be a powerful spiritual experience (and, at times, carefully included in a rite), there is no substitute for communal singing. Without the whole group singing, the ritual becomes merely a group reading or dialogue or act; this cannot build a community or nourish an individual within that community like singing together can.

We are capable of singing together, even if we don't do it often. Think of "Happy Birthday," Christmas carols, or a sports team fight song. A singer who is capable of leading others in song is helpful in encouraging the communal song. Each of the five rites in this book needs such a leader of singing.

In terms of what to sing, careful thought is needed beforehand. Some of the rites here suggest songs in place. Substitutions may be made when the community does not know or cannot learn the suggested song. But be careful! There's no benefit in substituting a non-scriptural song when a psalm or canticle is required, for example. Seek the advice of your parish music ministers for suggestions. Sometimes we know a psalm or song because we have sung it often at church, even if we may not remember having done so. The musical selections for these rituals, as well as many other beloved hymns and songs that might serve as worthy substitutes, are available for assembly usage via www.onelicense.net.

A Presider, One Who Leads, Is Needed

Each of these five rites requires a presider, one who leads the rite. This can be any man or woman with the necessary gifts and abilities. The presider knows the shape of the rite, and who is doing particular parts. So if, for example, a Scripture reader misses her or his cue, the presider can gently invite her or him without disturbing the atmosphere of prayer already established, and without embarrassing the reader. In addition to being able to read his or her parts, a good presider is one who can non-verbally direct the pace of the rite, so it is not rushed or unduly drawn out. A good presider can also invite a community to stand or sit without saying "Please stand" or "Please sit." A simple, graceful gesture can do that better, providing the presider knows the shape of the ritual.

Good Readers Are Indispensable

Proclaiming a passage from Scripture is best done by someone other than the presider. Obviously a reader must be one who can read in public loudly enough to be heard and with enough diction to be understood. But a good reader is one who reads the passage as many times as needed beforehand to be able to discern the messages that are being communicated. Then he or she uses the skills of public speaking to articulate that message to the gathering of people. Using a different reader for each Scripture passage is best. If the presider for any of these rites is not a priest or deacon, and a gospel passage has been selected for inclusion, it may be read by any reader, male or female.

*Blessing of Parents after a Miscarriage*

This is an official rite from the Roman Catholic *Book of Blessings*. A priest or deacon is the usual presider, so consider asking a priest or deacon from your parish to preside. But Church law allows for someone who is not ordained to preside when necessary.

As printed in this book, this rite requires a presider, and at least one reader. A person other than the presider may be chosen to lead the intercessions. While singing is not required, consider singing a song to begin and/or end the rite. This might then require providing a song sheet and a leader to begin each song.

# How *to* Use This Book

*Order for the Naming and Commendation of an Infant Who Died before Birth*

This is an official rite of the Archdiocese of St. Louis. A priest or deacon is the usual presider, so consider asking a priest or deacon from your parish to preside. But Church law allows for someone who is not ordained to preside when necessary.

A presider, a reader, and a leader of singing are needed.

Note that the parents of the deceased child have a part too, and be sure that they know what to do and that they are comfortable doing it.

*Liturgy of Remembrance*

Based on the *Blessing of Parents after a Miscarriage*, this ritual was adapted by a family member after the loss of an infant. As written, it has a priest presiding, but another may preside. It requires a reader for the gospel (if the presider is not a priest or deacon), another reader to lead the intercessions, and a leader of singing.

*Prayer with Siblings, Cousins, and Other Children*

This rite is deliberately designed for a parent to lead with children. As written, the parent is the only leader. But if that parent is not comfortable leading singing, another suitable person, even an older child, may be given that role. The song indicated in the ritual ("All Night, All Day") may be replaced by another suitable song that the children know.

# *Of* Womb *and* Tomb

*Evening Liturgy of the Word and Ritual of Light*

Here is an important lesson for the parish minister preparing a rite such as this: *What good habits does the parish already know and do that can be the basis of a new rite called for by this pastoral situation?*

This rite builds upon a long tradition of ritual prayer outside of Mass nourished at St. Nicholas in Evanston, Illinois. In this instance, three parish traditions of 12 years or more—monthly evening prayer celebrating a feast of the Lord or a woman doctor of the church, the annual All Souls Day Mass, and the annual November inscribing of names in the Book of Remembrance—prepared the assembly to gracefully do the ritual of light with a minimum of instruction. Singing the intercessions is the parish's longstanding custom on Sundays. All of the sung pieces are from the parish's repertoire, so nothing had to be taught before the rite began. Even though the "Lux aeterna" is used only once annually, its responsorial format combined with strong cantor leadership meant no rehearsal was needed.

As written, the liturgy is presided over by a priest. But another suitable person may preside and, depending on the local ordinary's rules, preach. The homily must be prepared and rehearsed most carefully, especially if the preacher does not preach regularly.

A minimum of four readers—five if the presider is not a priest or deacon—is needed: first reading, second reading, gospel, intercessions, names of the deceased children. The reader(s) of names must be comfortable with last-minute preparation, as the names are gathered just before the liturgy begins. A single reader may speak all the names, or two or three readers may take turns reading sections of names if the number of names allows. Lectors who lead the Sunday intercessions, with its last-minute list of names of the sick and the dead, are accustomed to doing this.

The second reading as printed here includes a refrain that the cantor leads and all sing. The reader needs to understand and be comfortable with this. It is also possible to distribute the parts of the reading to various readers. In the case of St. Nicholas, the parish was familiar with this practice from monthly evening prayer, where the singing of the second psalm included short pieces written by the saint of the day, or a commentary on the feast of the day, interspersed after the sung refrain of all.

People are invited to inscribe the names of their deceased children as they enter the worship space. If this rite is celebrated outside of November, consider using the parish's same ceremonial Book of Remembrance that is brought out each year. Having someone stationed by the book to make sure each name is legible helps. It's possible to ask for people to submit names in advance, but be ready to accommodate those who come who did not do so; it would be extremely unfortunate and perhaps "sour" someone on the church in the face of such inhospitality, however unintentional. As the liturgy begins, the reader(s) of names take the book to the sacristy and prepare themselves. An usher or minister of hospitality should be at the door to solicit any names brought by late-comers.

The liturgy ends with the sign of peace. Again, a good number of St. Nicholas parishioners would be familiar with this from evening prayer. In some instances, such an ending can seem awkward. This can be eased by printing a simple rubric on the song sheet, such as "All share a sign of peace as we end our prayer and take leave of each other this night." Or, if refreshments are served after, "All share a sign of peace as we end our prayer and go to [name of place] to share refreshments." The presider and all other ministers can facilitate this process by sharing the sign of peace as they make their way out of the assembly—a good nonverbal sign that the liturgy is completed.

**Appendix**

Included in the Appendix of this book is a homily given by Fr. Robert Oldershaw, pastor emeritus of St. Nicholas Church, at the first "Evening Liturgy of the Word and Ritual of Light" service. If there is a preaching element to the ritual, use this as an example of how to craft a message that is both sensitive and comforting.

**Book of Remembrance**

Many parishes and temples inscribe the names of those who have died in a ceremonial book or scroll. The Book of Daniel and the Book of Revelation both speak of God writing the names of loved ones on a scroll or in a book as a sign of the promise to never forget, to never give up on, to never lose a loved one, especially to death. In the Jewish tradition, remembering someone is a sacred act—it is the way that our loved ones live on, in our memories, in our hearts. Many congregations have a Book of Remembrance, where names of loved ones who have passed on can be inscribed, and writing their names there is a way to honor that memory. Catholic tradition devotes November to the remembering and celebrating of all the saints and souls who have gone before us, especially those who died in the past year.

Many Catholic parishes bring out a ceremonial book each November and invite people to inscribe the names of their beloved dead. One may even write the names in again each year. If you have experienced miscarriage or stillbirth, you may enter a name for your child who has died if this will help you grieve. It commends your child to God and to the whole community to remember.

You may begin a Book of Remembrance for your home, too. At the end of this book, we have begun a Book of Remembrance and included the names of the children of the contributors to this book who were lost before or at birth. Write the names of your loved ones who have died, including any children of your own or your friends, who died before or at birth. You may cut out this page or copy (by machine or by hand) the names here and insert them into a lovely blank book readily available online and in office supply stores. Display your Book of Remembrance in an honored place in your home: a fireplace mantel or on the sideboard in the dining room. You may want to also purchase a small easel to display it upright. Add some flowers and a candle. Perhaps the book is kept closed, but opened on November 2 each year (All Souls Day) and kept open until sunset on November 30. Or you might consider opening it on the night before the anniversary of the death of one of the persons whose name is inscribed, and keep it open until the next evening. This is a way of remembering this loved one, evening to evening.

If you are a parish minister, please inscribe the names included in the Book of Remembrance at the end of this book in your parish's ceremonial book. Seeing the way these entries are worded will serve as an invitation to others who have lost a child before or at birth to inscribe those names too.

# WITH GRATITUDE

For the women and men whose stories appear in this resource: Susan Reynolds, Robert Kim Williams, Karen Girolami Callam, Timothy P. O'Malley, Megan Kennedy-Farrell.

For the women and men who shared with me their experiences, hopes, and dreams, and helped me to understand what might be important; for Carolina Gomez, Melissa Rupp, Sally Clark Arden, Janice Williams.

For Laura Kelly Fanucci, for her willingness to dialogue with me about her own journey, for the gift of her ability to articulate through writing, and for the incredible work that she and her husband, Franco David Fanucci, have done creating *Grieving Together: A Couple's Journey through Miscarriage*. (Our Sunday Visitor: Huntington IN)

For Ace Gangoso, John Schuchert, Sue Garthwaite, and the community of St. Nicholas Church in Evanston, Illinois, for the courage and care shown in offering opportunities for prayer that provide a much needed light in the darkness, working to shape us as Christ's presence for one another.

For Melissa Carnall, and all who work as chaplains and ministers, accompanying those grieving in hospitals and in their homes; for all who work to find words and presence to bring comfort and healing.

For David Philippart, for his liturgical expertise, for his dedication to and capacity for compassion, for his wisdom, and for his belief in what is possible when we pray.

For Tony Alonso, a great friend and mentor, who challenges and invites me to think deeply, to love the Church that we are called to serve, and to have hope in God who works in us to bring light and hope to the world.

For Alec Harris and the incredible team of composers, authors, and editors at GIA Publications, Inc., who make possible our vision to bring to life the song that carries us when words alone cannot.

For my husband, Scott, faithful companion at my side through all the seasons of life.

For my daughter, Ava, who taught me about the God of Surprises early in the womb.

# SACRED STORIES

# VIGIL-KEEPING

## SUSAN REYNOLDS, PhD

*Can a mother forget her infant?*
*Be without tenderness for the child of her womb?*
*Even should she forget,*
*I will never forget you.*

The words of the lectionary fell on me like acid: a raw, electric sting. It felt like someone had ripped off a layer of my skin.

I suffered my first miscarriage, and the two that followed it, when I was a young graduate student in theology. That morning, four days after I started to bleed, I dragged myself out of my small apartment and into the icy chill of early March in Boston, numbly heeding my dad's advice to somehow business-as-usual my way back to life. Seeking consolation, I drifted into weekday Mass in the school's chapel. I sunk into a seat at the end of a row, next to a colleague whose glance in my direction—a mixture of horror and pity—suggested to me that I looked like some kind of disheveled ghost.

My body felt to me like a collection of metaphors torn from the pages of the psalms. Life was pouring out of me like water. My mouth had dried up like a sandy shard of pottery; my heart had melted like wax and re-hardened as a formless mass in the base of my chest. Dried tears formed salty deltas at the creases of my eyes. I was a pile of bones, a living tomb, alive yet containing death itself.

*Can a mother forget her infant?*

In that moment, the words of Isaiah felt cruelly ironic. It seemed to me that the world was engaged in a conspiracy to make me forget the child who, for two buoyant months, I had carried under my heart.

At the hospital, the doctor had confirmed my miscarriage in the voice of someone commenting on the weather in another state. She told me my world was shattered through sips of her fountain soda and a casual shrug. She told me I could go. I stared at her. *Go where?* I wondered.

In the realm of women's experience, the mandate to forget is magisterial. Pregnant women are typically cautioned to wait until their second trimester, after the risk of miscarriage has declined, to tell others that they are expecting. Implicitly contained within this well-meaning advice is the expectation of forgetting. If you have a miscarriage, the age-old wisdom seems to convey, the right thing to do is never to tell anyone about the child you carried and lost. Instead, you should go on with life as though nothing has happened and never speak of it again. In any other circumstance, we would find such advice monstrous. As it is, women's bodily experiences of loss are shuffled off to the attic of daily life, hidden firmly from sight like the senile spinster aunt in a Victorian novel.

Over generations, the stream of imposed forgetting slowly erodes the bedrock of communal experience. Where we should find a mountain—memories upon memories, stories upon stories, rituals upon rituals—we encounter instead a gaping canyon, a tradition of absence. Miscarriage is a phenomenon as intrinsic to the human condition as birth and death. Yet the unique grief that unfolds in the mysterious space in between life and death remains unspoken, even within families and among close friends. My mother had suffered several miscarriages. So, as it turned out, had my husband's mother, his aunts, and a sizeable proportion of the women I knew. I knew none of this at the time. I knew nothing about what had happened to them, so I knew nothing about what was happening to me. How did they grieve? What did they do with their babies' remains? How did they heal? What did they do to remember?

In the liturgy, *anamnesis* is the Greek term given to ritual words and actions of remembrance. When we celebrate the Eucharist, we remember Jesus' suffering, death, and resurrection in a way that forms us into a community of memory and hope. Liturgical remembering is an act of truth-telling. It is a way of saying: *This is our story. This is where we have come from. This is the living God in whose image we were formed and by whose love we are saved.* I often think of the repetitive nature of Catholic liturgical participation as a kind of vigil-keeping. Deep in this relentless remembering, this protest against forgetting God's work of salvation, is rooted our hope.

Within the Catholic liturgical and sacramental tradition, few rituals exist to mark the hidden loss of miscarriage. Often neither baptism nor funeral suffice; yet still we believe that these tiny lives have meaning. As women, our bodies are the sites of their memory. Our flesh bears witness to their having lived. When children die in the womb, they leave little material evidence of their existence. The fleeting, ambiguous nature of their lives is, in part, what makes prenatal loss so bitter and unspeakable. It is also what makes the communal act of remembering them so vital. Indeed, their memories make a claim upon us and upon the entire community. As personal as the experience of prenatal loss is, the exclusion of these stories from public consciousness serves only to compound grief with isolation.

Indeed, after a month of hazy, directionless mourning in the wake of my first miscarriage, I realized that what I longed for was ritual—a prayerful space of mourning and healing within the life-giving embrace of my community. My husband and I planned a bilingual liturgy of remembrance at our parish, along with a Jesuit friend and a fellow parishioner from the Spanish Mass community who had also recently suffered a miscarriage. We welcomed all families who had ever lost a child in the womb or who wanted to pray for someone who had. When the evening of the liturgy arrived, we were astounded to find that the gathering overflowed our small parish's chapel. Women came who had lost babies years and even decades before. As we prayed together, they cried tears as fresh as my own. "I have carried this pain in my heart for more than half my life," one woman told me later that night. "I never had anyone to tell. I never had any place to go to remember."

The mandate to forget had not worked. The veil of silence had not served. The memories of our babies lived, unburied and raw. At the conclusion of the service, we invited those gathered to light a candle for each child they had lost. As we named our children in the presence of God and one another, in unity with the entire communion of saints, we found ourselves enfolded in the tender mercy of God—the God who remembers our cries as a mother remembers the children who are flesh of her flesh. Together, we laid our candles before the altar, at the feet of an image of Our Lady of Guadalupe. The memories of our children, once hidden, now illuminated the darkened chapel.

*Susan B. Reynolds, PhD, is Assistant Professor of Catholic Studies at Emory University's Candler School of Theology in Atlanta. She and her husband Drew have two young daughters.*

---

# Our First Baby

## Robert Kim Williams

It was the summer of our dreams. Janice and I were returning from a three-week trip to Europe. Coming home to our small central Illinois town with stories to tell, we found that our most important story was waiting. Janice was pregnant with our first child.

It was 1982, four years after our wedding day. We each had busy careers—I was a newspaper reporter and Janice was a special education teacher. We both had a wide circle of friends, and weekends were not often spent at home. Bringing a child into the world was definitely not an afterthought; we both wanted to have children. During those early years of marriage, being alone with each other just seemed more comfortable. But now the yearning for a child had begun.

The Europe trip had been a breakout adventure. We traveled by coach bus through eight countries as part of a university-sponsored tour. We were one of two married couples on our bus; it was a wonderful mix of college-age students and older adults getting that chance to explore Europe. It happened to be a World Cup summer; the excitement on the continent was ramped up because three of the final four teams were European. When Italy won the Cup, we saw their fans celebrate in droves where we were—in Brussels.

Not long after we returned home, Janice brought me the news she was pregnant, and we shared it with great joy. It was one of the important things God had given us—the ability through Him to bring home a new life. The thrill was overwhelming. We were preparing ourselves to become parents.

We kiddingly called the little one our "Brussels sprout," since we had spent the last week of our European trip in Belgium's capital city and felt like the baby might have been conceived there. Janice had started wearing maternity clothes; the pregnancy was nearing four months.

Then one night, the excitement and anticipation were shattered. Janice began to have severe cramps. They grew worse and we felt it was time to head to the ER. In our small town, it was a short trip. But then, Janice miscarried at home.

In the next few days, my feelings of horror at losing our baby to a miscarriage turned to deep sadness. We had become a mommy and daddy, but now with no baby to love and hold close.

What could we do, what if we tried again? And this happened again! How strong was I, really? My sadness for Janice was more than I could bear. She felt the awful pain and then this tiny ray of light slipped away. At the time of our baby's death, it was customary to test the remains and then dispose of "the tissue." We were saddened when we found this out.

"*C'mon God! What's the deal? We're loyal churchgoers; we put our trust in you! How could this happen?*"

Even though I just wrote those thoughts, I really didn't feel that way. Although I am no saint, I didn't feel that was the way to react. Janice and I were aware of the risks involved with carrying and delivering a child. Just because you love and trust God in the name of His Son Jesus Christ, it doesn't mean you are entitled to a life free of grief and pain. But in fact God did *not* abandon us, even along the rough stretch of road ahead.

Word spreads fast in a small town and many of the words that came our way were far from comforting. "It's for the better" or "It's God's will" were some of the comments. And there were other careless remarks: "You're young, you can always get pregnant again." "This must not have been the right time." "It's nature's way; there must have been something wrong with the baby." "This happens to a lot of women." Or one real head-scratcher: "You two are so busy; you just need to relax."

*"Thank you for those ridiculous sentiments meant to be words of comfort"* were the thoughts screaming in our heads as we politely nodded each time and walked away.

Following the miscarriage, Janice's doctor told her the tests showed the baby would have been a girl. He wanted Janice to wait six months before trying again, if we felt strong enough to try. During that time, it was difficult for us to be around babies and go to baby showers. We were happy for the new parents, but these times also brought back the pain. It was also difficult to answer insensitive, personal questions like, "When are you going to try again?"

Our spirits were really hitting the low points, but at the same time God was sending true comforters to us in the person of women in the community who had lost babies to miscarriage or stillbirth. Individually, the women, guided by the Holy Spirit, came alongside Janice, gently confiding that they had gone through a similar trauma. Not only were there words of comfort, there were flowers, sympathy cards, meals, quiet visits, or simply a wordless hug.

We knew that those who clumsily tried to comfort us with the wrong words did it without malice. We also learned that comforting the grieving is as easy as a warm hug and an ear willing to listen. People need to realize that they don't have all the answers to the bad things that happen to others. Although many are convinced otherwise, people are *not* all-knowing. That's God's department.

The words and gestures that brought us comfort came from those who knew that showing up and standing beside a grieving couple was a step toward healing. Sometimes just being there or quietly asking, "What can I do to help your family" is all that's needed at the time.

Our terrors eased up; we felt some peace. This had been like running the gauntlet, but now, we grew close.

On November 27, 1983, Robert Christopher Williams checked into the world. Scott Patrick Williams joined the family on May 16, 1986. And on May 31, 1990, Alex Michael Williams made us the latest version of "My Three Sons."

Even with three very lively boys lighting up our house, we never forgot our first baby. For the first couple years afterward, we bought a tiny angel each year to place on the Christmas tree. Then something happened that helped us to see this loss in a new way. The daughter of one of Janice's fellow teachers lost a baby to stillbirth. This wonderful young woman addressed her grief and helped other women facing the same trauma by researching ways to remember the child through a variety of memorials, such as planting a tree, starting a memorial garden or holding a special service. A booklet she gave to Janice led us to the next step.

Eight years after our baby's death, following Alex's baptism, we held a memorial service for the baby that we knew had to be named—because Christ knows the names of all his sheep. We had referred to her the past eight years by her name, not "the miscarriage."

Her name is Kelley Lynn Williams: Kelley is the maiden name of Janice's mother and Lynn is Janice's middle name.

How did this ceremony—having a service and naming a child who did not make it to childbirth—affect our family? I have to point to the two no-nonsense grandfathers. Janice's father, Bert, the Caterpillar engineer who served in the Pacific during World War II, wept. My father, Doc Williams, the local veterinarian who helped bring all kinds of animals into the world, was visibly moved. Other family members wept with tears of remembrance, hope, or peace.

As we gathered for brunch afterward, the mood was joyful. Joy for Alex's baptism and joy for God's loving hand in connecting us all to Kelley Lynn's short life on earth.

There seemed to be closure for all of us—parents, brothers, grandparents, aunts and uncles. This child whom we never met and who departed before we even knew her? Now she had a name.

We will see you again, Kelley Lynn . . .

*The one who enters by the gate is the shepherd of the sheep. The gatekeeper opens the gate for him, and the sheep listen to his voice. He calls his own sheep by name and leads them out. When he has brought out all his own, he goes on ahead of them, and his sheep follow him because they know his voice.*

*John 10:2–4, NIV*

*Robert Kim Williams is a journalist, with forty-two years as a reporter and an editor in the newspaper industry. He is married to Janice and they are the parents of three grown sons: Christopher, Scott, and Alex.*

# YES, I AM WHOLE

## KAREN GIROLAMI CALLAM

*October 26, 2006*
*I am five weeks and five days pregnant. It's so completely NOT sinking*
*in that it's downright bizarre. It feels entirely hypothetical. My body is*
*in cahoots with my brain and giving me next to no symptoms yet...*
*But supposedly, somehow, unbelievably, incredulously, there is a baby*
*growing inside me. Cells multiplying furiously... Is this truly our third*
*child in the making?*

Triana, our 5-year-old, was playing her first soccer games that fall, encouraged by her papa and my husband, Coach Kirby. Well, she watched more than played, unsure at first, but gradually warmed to it. Kindergarten started with teary goodbyes that faded to confident hugs and waves. Her interest in reading and writing exploded. She was crazy about her younger brother.

Santiago was 3 and obsessed with distinguishing good from evil. Whales, dolphins, sharks: "Which is scary? Which eat people?" Every night at bedtime: "¿Vienen monstruos o truenos?" (monsters or thunder). He loved drama, and we loved his sense of humor. One day he told me God was in his heart. "Listen, Mama," he said, pulling me close. "GRRRrrrrr!" he growled and I jumped back, startled, as he giggled with delight.

Just twenty-two months apart, they were in each other's space constantly, with love and frustration. Triana would scold him as they played dress-up, "Ay-yay-yay, Santi!" He'd respond, "No! Ay-yay-yay, tú!"

It was intense and wonderful, life with two small kids. We'd married in our mid-30s and prioritized becoming parents. At our pre-wedding retreat, I wrote down my marriage goals: "1. Have a child. 2. Have a second child." Kirby loved to good-naturedly needle me for that, but it was true: mothering was—and is—the center of my being.

Kirby taught middle school math; I was part-time communications consultant to nonprofits and schools, part-time singer/music teacher. We were raising our kids bilingually and dreamed of moving our family to Spain, where I had lived in college and again in my 20s. We wanted the kids to have a full immersion experience. We wanted a family adventure, to stretch ourselves, and were open to the unknowns it would bring. Was this the moment to make it happen?

We also deeply wanted another baby. We felt we had a lot to offer as parents. But I was also 40. I felt strong and healthy, ready but wary, disbelieving that, after talking about it, shelving it, then talking about it again, we were at this moment actually pregnant.

*November 16, 2006*
*Our consciousness has a big day tomorrow: our first appointment with our dear midwife. Our first chance to verify this, perhaps hear a heartbeat, catch a glimpse? We are hungry—I know I am ravenous—for some sign of life beyond slight nausea here, slight tiredness there, heavier breasts… I am full of doubts and questions, hopes and fears, longing to know this creature and what it means for us.*

I re-read these journal entries now and wonder: was my disbelief a sixth sense that this pregnancy wouldn't last? It was a heady visit. We heard the galloping heartbeat during that first ultrasound: familiar, jubilant. But the hormone levels in my blood tests weren't good and at a return visit a week later: no heartbeat.

We were stunned, quiet, so, so, sad. But practical too, which is the gift and curse of having older children. I had to move forward. I had the option of a D&C procedure or waiting it out. After two pregnancies and natural childbirths, I felt confident and in sync with my body. I trusted it would know what to do, and be strong enough to do it. I wondered if I could handle knowing this baby was inside me, but no longer alive. Would its journey out take hours or days?

I decided to wait. A couple days later during Sunday Mass, as I stood with my choir and sang Bob Moore's soothingly beautiful song "All Glory Is Yours," I felt a rush of warm ache and, suddenly, an emptying out. I made it to the bathroom, into the ready arms of Kirby, and the loving efficiency of my family nurse practitioner. She found towels. Somehow I got home.

*December 24, 2006*

*I am desperately wakeful lately—clinging to life in the quiet hours of night, looking for peace in the stillness, brain too busy to shut down. I swing from sadness to deep melancholy to steady resolve to deep confusion. So much has happened since one month ago, when we heard no heartbeat, saw no baby, and then were awash in a sea of blood and tissue and tears for days on end as I miscarried. I have wanted and needed to write but haven't found the focus amidst the physical turmoil, then the emotional wringing, followed by the furiously busy December. I have felt essentially alone in all this, although friends and even a few acquaintances have offered empathy, support, shared sorrow. Miscarriage is so common, so isolating, so lonely, so complete, such a setback, and so weirdly unsettling. Now we march into Christmas, a Christmas I would have been pregnant. Kirby seems detached, somewhere in his own sorrow, or just not attending to it, nor to mine. I must keep looking inside me, and the music, for some peace to persevere.*

Music is a place of peace for me. Without singing, I would never have come back to church as an adult, so the fact that I miscarried while singing in church makes perfect sense. But the physical event went on and on, over days. Each woman's miscarriage is unique; this one, for me, was really drawn-out. A couple days later, when my doctor lifted a small piece of tissue off my cervix, and my uterus finally stopped contracting, the physical event finally ended.

But the emotional event continued. And for however much I loved our progressive, welcoming church community, and felt known and loved by at least a handful of people there, I was still essentially alone. My miscarriage—a miscarriage that happened IN CHURCH—was still essentially a private event. Hush-hush over the pain, don't-ask about the process.

I realize that's, in part, respect for privacy, for the intimacy of the experience. But it was also about our lack of rituals—public and private—to recognize this common experience in the circle of life.

What might it have been like if, in a moment when I felt ready, there would have been a way to recognize the pain and the process within my own faith community? What if we had lifted our voices' healing power together? I'll never know. But I can imagine it: a safe, spiritual space for women and their families, friends, and community to say and know, "Yes, this happened. Yes, God is here too. Yes, I am whole."

Life did go on, in all sorts of unexpected ways. Over the winter, we lifted our gazes towards hope once again, got pregnant again, and miscarried again. It was an incredibly different event, earlier in the pregnancy this time, and also deeply sad. It happened fast, at home, over dinner. I was overcome with full body shakes, and in a long tremor, it was over. Reeling, for days, weeks, I looked for logic. It didn't make sense. How could it? My strong, healthy body—really? Again? Yes, really, my midwife assured me: two miscarriages in a row weren't so uncommon.

Again my body knew more than my mind. Again I trusted and leaned on family and a few friends. Again my faith community was largely unaware. Kind gestures—mostly from women friends who had experienced this too—were comforting: a couple meals, cards, even a small prayer book from our Director of Liturgy, who had heard the news from a friend.

One written sentiment stopped me cold and continues to be a lighthouse in storms for me: the idea that women all over the world experience incredible pain and hardship for all sorts of reasons, and that my experience was now a connection that I had with them, a bond of understanding.

Early pregnancy, miscarriage, and loss is often our secret as women. Society tells us (and we tell ourselves) that it's not time to tell, it's not right to share these glories and tragedies. Or we simply don't have a way or a place, beyond our circle of closest ones. There's random processing that brings its own gifts. We end up sharing these experiences not with the *best* person, but with the best person *at the moment*: the person who happens to be standing outside school, the one who walks by your house when you're crying, someone you meet at a conference.

These moments bring blessings, but we need more. We need rituals that provide some place to hold the emotion of the moment, that provide a place for us to be held, by those who love us, by those who simply feel connected to us through the pain, by the arms of God in the form of our faith community.

I moved forward. I held the emotional weight of the loss, but with a sense of practicality, even in my saddest moments. We had two small kids, work, lots of things going on. Who doesn't?

But it was more than distraction. It was strength. I felt a strength in embracing my losses, rather than a brokenness from them. This strength carried me, and Kirby too, I think. But it was largely private. There weren't rituals for the sadness or for the strength.

So much of loss is losing the *idea*: the *idea* of another baby, of a sibling for Triana and Santi. That's in part how we knew this chapter in our lifebook wasn't all written yet. We couldn't let go of this idea. Despite painful comments from our families conveying, "No more tries, right?" we opened ourselves once again to possibility. We got pregnant again, disbelieved again, and were surprised once again. By Gemma, who's now 10 and the emotional center of our family.

Not long after my miscarriages, a friend faced her own string of sorrows, miscarrying again and again. I wrote to her: *Your family story will continue to unfold and be yours and yours alone. Not that it always will make sense. Ours continues to surprise us. Doors close. Windows open. In the midst of the most confusing pain, one of the kids will do or say something that brings deep delight. And that is all you will have. And it will be everything you need, in that moment.*

*Karen Girolami Callam is a writer, singer, and teacher. Her bilingual communications consultancy focuses on telling the stories of nonprofits, schools, and foundations. She also teaches music and movement classes to young children. Karen lives in Evanston, Illinois, with her husband Kirby and their three children.*

# Waiting *for* Gabriel

## Timothy P. O'Malley, PhD

"Do you have children?" For most 30-somethings, this harmless question is the opening volley of a round of acceptable chit-chat. Colleagues at the office fill silences with news of recent pregnancies, first Communions and athletic milestones in their children's lives. At the barbershop, the shearing of hair is accompanied by regaling the barber with mundane details of one's progeny. College reunions become an occasion not simply to reminisce about chemistry class or the bizarre rituals of freshman orientation, but to meet the miniature version of the guy down the hall, who once set up a slip-and-slide on the quad when the temperature climbed above 50 degrees.

For my wife and me, however, a question about our brood never offers an escape route from awkward social interactions, but is rather the prelude to uncomfortable conversations with strangers and confidants alike. "No children," we say, our voices revealing our discomfort with the question. How can you say to a complete stranger, a trusted teacher, a friendly cleric, a college classmate: "We're infertile"?

In the Old Testament, Hannah gives birth to Samuel after years of infertility and sings, "The barren wife bears seven sons, while the mother of many languishes" (1 Samuel 2:5). As a theologian, I am well aware of the function of infertility in the Scriptures. When the aged Sarah, the elderly Hannah and the mature Elizabeth give birth, the reader is invited to remember that God is the major actor in salvation. The surprising reversal of infertility in the Bible is a sign of new life coming from death, an action made possible by God, who is the creator and sustainer of human life. But that part of me who has spent the last six years praying for a child cannot help but read Hannah's song as a cry of relief. After years of barrenness and tears, finally a child!

When my wife and I were first married, we never imagined that we might join the ranks of Abraham and Sarah, Elkanah and Hannah, Elizabeth and Zechariah. We met before our senior year at the University of Notre Dame and became engaged a little over a year after we began to date. Like so many Notre Dame couples before us, our nuptials took place at the university's Basilica of the Sacred Heart, where the priest prayed over us: "Bless them with children and help them to be good parents. May they live to see their children's children." In our first year of marriage in Boston, we decided it was time to begin a family. Month one passed. Month two. Month three. Six months later, our home became the anti-Nazareth as we awaited an annunciation that never came. The hope-filled decision to conceive a child became a bitter task of disheartened waiting. After a year, we began to see infertility specialists, who concluded that we should be able to have a child. No low sperm counts. No problems with either of our reproductive systems. The verdict: inexplicable infertility.

Unexplained infertility is a surprisingly miserable diagnosis. Something about my psyche was prepared for a scientific explanation—one in which our very fine doctors acknowledged that unless an act of God took place, no human life would emerge from intercourse between Kara and me. Indeed, a fair number of tears would have been shed by both of us. But with the diagnosis of inexplicable infertility, conception is scientifically possible. With every slight change in Kara's cycle, a glimmer of hope rises in our hearts, only to be dashed with the arrival of menstruation. Kind-hearted family, friends, and colleagues who learn about our infertility share stories about a mother or sister who finally became pregnant. But we have no way of knowing if we will one day join the ranks of the middle-aged, first-time parents.

The aftermath of the diagnosis was painful for both of us. It affected not simply our friendships and our own relationship, but also our spiritual lives. Our infertility gradually seeped into our life of prayer. Every morning, I rise and ask God for a child. I encounter the chilly silence of a seemingly absent God. Early on I found consolation in the language of the psalms, "My God, my God, why have you abandoned me?" (Psalm 22:2). Like the psalmist, I had my "enemies": the friendly priest, who, upon learning that Kara and I do not have children, made it a point to say each time he saw me, "No children, right?"; the Facebook feed filled with announcements of pregnancies and births, a constant reminder of our empty nest. Even God became my nemesis: Why have you duped me, O Lord? Why us? We have given our lives to you, and our reward is pain and suffering.

Such self-pity, while pleasant enough for a time, is exhausting and a sure way to narcissism. We began to imagine that ours was the only life full of disappointment. We closed ourselves off from relationships with others, particularly those with children, as a way of protecting ourselves from debilitating sorrow. I ceased praying, because the words I uttered grew vapid, insipid, uninspiring. I entered Sheol, cut off from the land of the living. Something had to change.

How did I escape this hell? First, I learned to give myself over to a reality beyond my control. Life is filled with any number of things that happen to us. We are diagnosed with illnesses. Our family, despite our love, falls apart because of fighting among siblings over how to handle the remaining years of a parent's life. We die. The beginning of true Christian faith is in trusting that even in such moments, God abides with us. This God invites us to offer our sorrow, our very woundedness, as an act of love. As Pierre

Teilhard de Chardin, SJ, wrote in *The Divine Milieu*:

> Christ has conquered death, not only by suppressing its evil effects, but by reversing its sting. By virtue of Christ's rising again, nothing any longer kills inevitably, but everything is capable of becoming the blessed touch of the divine hands, the blessed influence of the will of God upon our lives.... For those loving God, all things are converted into good.

Praying the psalms again was the beginning of my own conversion toward the good. I learned that in uttering these words from a wounded heart, my voice became Christ's. My suffering, my sorrow has been whispered into the ear of the Father for all time. The echo of my words in an empty room called my heart back to authentic prayer. Whenever I was tempted to enter into self-pity, I used short phrases from the psalms to bring myself back toward the Father. The psalms became the grammar of my broken speech to God.

Second, I began to meditate upon the crucifix whenever I entered a church. Gazing at the crucifix for long periods, I discovered how God's silence in my prayer was stretching me toward more authentic love. In contemplating the silence of the cross, the image of Christ stretched out in love, I could feel my own will stretched out gradually to exist in harmony with the Father's, to accept the cup that we have been given. I found new capacities for love available to me. I became especially attentive to the suffering of the widow, the immigrant, the lonely and all those who come to Mass with a wounded heart. My meditation upon the image of the cross has given me the strength to go forward with the process of adoption and foster care. The cross sustains me as Kara and I continue to wait for a child, who may need more love than we could ever imagine giving.

Third, in my formation into prayer through infertility, I have grown to appreciate the silence and half-sentences of God. Often, words still hurt too much for me to utter. In such sorrow, I have no energy in prayer. All I have left is an imitation of the very silence I hear in response to my petitions. Through entering into God's own silence, I find my own bitterness transformed into trust and hope, a kind of infused knowledge of God's love that I have come to savor. At times, albeit rarely, this silence results in a gift of exhilarating bliss—as if for a moment, I am totally united to God. Most often, it is a restful silence in which I hear no words. I savor such moments because only here do I receive the balm for the sorrow that often floods my soul throughout the day.

Fourth, our infertility has slowly led me to a deeper appreciation of the eucharistic quality of the Christian life. For years, I talked with far too much ease about the "sacrifice of the Mass"—how all of our lives must become an offering, a gift to the Father through the Son in the unity of the Holy Spirit. In fact, true self-gift is hard. It is hard to give yourself away to a God who does not seem to listen to your prayers. It is hard to wait for a child who may never come. It is hard to love your spouse when you are distracted by the phantasms of sorrow that have become your dearest friend. It is hard to muster a smile when your friends announce that they will be having another child. It is just hard.

At such moments, I do not know what else to do but to seek union with Christ himself; to enter more deeply into the eucharistic logic of the church, where self-preservation is transformed into self-gift. The Eucharist continues to teach me that I cannot do it myself. I cannot climb out of the sorrow, the sadness, the misery. But I can give it away. I can slowly enter into the eucharistic life of the church, to become vulnerable, self-giving love even in the midst of sorrow. Knowing, of course, that in the Resurrection, such love has conquered death.

As I have learned most of all through the Eucharist, Kara and I were not married for ourselves. We were married that our lives might become an offering of love for the world. For our nieces, for our nephews, for a child not biologically our own but whom we hope one day to welcome. Even our infertility is not about us. It's about how God can transform our sorrow into joy, how even in the shadow of this cross, the light shines in the darkness and the darkness will not overcome it. Of course, our woundedness remains. But prayer has given it a shape, a reason, a participation in God's very life. Even through this suffering, the Word desires to become flesh in my life through a prayerful obedience to the will of a God whom I cannot quite comprehend.

Sometimes I allow myself to daydream about having a child. I recognize now that such a moment may never come, that nothing in human life is sure. That is why learning to pray through infertility has been a reformation of my vision of grace as gift, not guarantee. If grace were guaranteed, would such moments be grace, a gift beyond what we could imagine? So we stand waiting for Gabriel, learning to hear the angel's voice in new ways: in time spent with our godchildren, in signing up to serve as foster parents, in delighting in each other's presence. And the more I enter into the grace of prayer, the more I see that Gabriel has already come in these moments: Let it be done to me according to your word.

*Timothy P. O'Malley, PhD, is the director of education at the McGrath Institute for Church Life and a professor of theology at the University of Notre Dame. He is married to Kara and has two young children.*

---

# Naming You

## Megan Kennedy-Farrell

It had been nearly a year since I lost you—a year of incredible grief and emptiness. Now it was Good Friday and as I sat in the darkness of my beloved church, next to your father and my partner in this life and grief, I heard these familiar words, *They took the body of Jesus and wrapped it with the spices in linen cloths, according to the burial custom of the Jews.* But this year they had new meaning. I was overcome and began to sob. *This,* I thought. *This is all I wanted.* I wanted to wrap you in spiced linens and bury you in a place I could return to. In a place that was sacred and everlasting.

--------------------------------------------------

I was on vacation with friends in New Mexico when I first suspected you were with me. Something felt different—I felt different. I stood in the Georgia O'Keeffe Museum and looked at a painting of the Pedernal Mountain. Something in the way she had painted the blue sky looked like a womb to me. I knew. I bought the children's book *My Name Is Georgia* in the museum gift shop. One day I would read it to you and tell you about the first moment I knew you.

But that day was not to be. At our first appointment, three weeks later, filled with anticipation and excitement, we heard: *There is a fetal pole, but no heartbeat. Maybe your dates are wrong.* (I knew they weren't.) *You will start to bleed... could be tomorrow, could be two weeks from now... it will be like a heavy period... go to the emergency room if you soak more than a pad an hour... Take your time leaving...* She hurried uncomfortably out the door, leaving your Dad and me alone and stunned, staring at the now blank ultrasound screen.

I did start to bleed, two days later. And it went on for days. Days and days of light spotting. After more than a week of this, and with no other information on what to expect, I went back to work thinking this was it. But a few days later, between meetings, I stopped at home. I had a few minutes and decided I would just lie down. I didn't feel well. Then the cramps got stronger and the bleeding got heavy and I got scared. I had left my cell phone on my desk at work. I couldn't reach your Dad. I was alone in the bathroom, and my body was doing something it had never done before.

After some time—I don't know how long—I was sweating and shaking and there was a lot of blood, but I was able to leave the bathroom and return to bed. Your beautiful, loving Dad returned home. I was sleeping, but the scene in the bathroom told him all he needed to know. When I woke up, the cramps had subsided, the bleeding had nearly ceased, and with the bathroom now cleaned up, you were gone.

You were gone and I was forever changed. There was nothing left of you to wrap or to bury. The only concrete evidence I had of your having existed was *My Name Is Georgia,* the book I would never get to read to you.

I have always hated the word miscarriage. It feels so full of blame and, while my head can understand the science, my heart cries out to you and all of my babies (six of them now): *I'm so sorry I miscarried you, that I couldn't carry you stronger, that I couldn't hold you tighter.* But I did carry you strong. I did hold you tight. In all of my miscarriages, my body held on for days and weeks after your hearts stopped beating. Friends, nurses and midwives always offered (sometimes strongly encouraged) the option of speeding the process along. But, I never wanted that. I wanted to carry you for every minute that I could. I wanted to be with you for each moment that I had. I wanted to bring your life to its final completion.

Three months after I lost you, I had the chance to sit with a dear friend who is also a wise, faith-filled, deeply spiritual woman. At the time, she was a new mom to twin boys. I didn't know that she was also the mom to another boy. A boy she had named Francis. A boy she had lost the year before when she was fourteen weeks pregnant. Before this conversation, I hadn't known I could name you, my child. Hardly anyone in the world even knew you had existed. I thought that was just how it was. But now I knew. I could name you. But what name would honor you and your life as it had *actually* been? Who were you?

Francis' mom had not only named her baby, but she had buried him in a beautiful cemetery near her home. She had demanded that the hospital let her keep his remains and found a sacred place for him to rest eternally—a place where she first brought him flowers and later introduced him to his brothers. He and she had a place in the world that remembered him. And that Good Friday, sitting in the darkened church, hearing the words of the Gospel of John, I grieved for the chance I did not have to wrap your tiny body, not yet fully formed, with my loving touch and lay you to rest. I grieved for a place in the world that would remember you.

I laid in bed days after this visit thinking of you, dreaming of you and suddenly I knew. I could not go back and change all that had been. But I could name you. Terese—your name would be Terese. The minute the name came to me, I knew it was yours and I felt my relationship deepen with you immediately. I knew you in a new way and I felt my first moment of peace.

St. Terese the Little Flower had said she would "spend her heaven doing good on earth." I had longed for you. I felt shattered that you were gone. But deep inside, beneath all the pain, I knew you had already done good on earth. I knew your soul had mysteriously added to the wonder and perfection of my world, of our world. I knew you would journey with me, each day that was ahead. And you have.

I clung to you when, fifteen long months after losing you, I was finally pregnant again and terrified of another loss. I felt your presence through an endless on again, off again labor when I was still afraid I would not bring this baby into full life. You were there in the beautiful roses your Dad bought for your perfectly healthy sister—a first gift to her, so she would always know of you, our little flower.

I called to you two years later when we heard the devastating words: *This* was *a twin pregnancy. But, I am sorry, there are no heartbeats.* I held you close when, that All Souls Day, my body let go of these babies, too. And I felt your soul and spirit with us as we planned to bury them in the way we didn't get to with you.

A friend had recently given me a beautiful metal angel, made by artisans in the Sudanese town where she was living. The angel was the gift, but it came in a small woven box that I had found so beautiful and had kept. Your dad and I laid the remains of our precious twins in this box. We covered them with cloth leftover from the baptismal gown your Nana had made for your sister out of my first Communion dress. We buried Julian Elizabeth and Gabriel Thomas in the center of our garden and covered them with rose petals in honor of our little flower, Terese.

Today, to the outside world, we are a family of four in seemingly perfect symmetry: Mom, Dad, sister, brother. But we, and those closest to us, know. We see the ever-present angels who surround us. Terese, Gabriel Thomas, Julian Elizabeth, Aine, Bridgid, and Daniel Joseph—you are our angels and saints, our "friends of God and prophets." Your lives, however fleeting, changed ours in profound ways. I would do anything to have even one of you here, living on this earth with us—to hear the sound of your voice and know the touch of your hand—to see the world through your unique eyes. But I wouldn't want to never have known you. Each one of you taught me profound lessons of hope and acceptance, of suffering and grief. Each one of you carved out space in my heart. Because of you, I journey differently in this world. I hope to honor your lives and your memory each day that I live. I love you.

Forever.

*Megan Kennedy-Farrell is the Senior Director of Mission and Identity at Solidarity Bridge in Evanston, Illinois. She is married to John and they have two living children.*

---

# POEMS, HYMNS, *and* BLESSINGS

**AND JESUS SAID:** don't be afraid—
I've come to turn your fear to hope,
I've come to take you through the deep,
    to be your friend
    until the end,
and give your troubled heart to sleep.

And Jesus said: don't be afraid—
I know your emptiness and grief,
I hear your words of unbelief,
    but if you will,
    I'll heal your soul
and give your doubting heart relief.

And Jesus said: don't be afraid—
I am the Way, I am the Light,
I am the Truth that holds you tight,
    and in God's home
    you have a room,
a place of welcome and delight.

Shirley Erena Murray

Meter: 8 8 8 4 4 8
*A musical setting of this hymn text is available,* G-7075.

**I** KNOW
that when the stress has grown too strong,
  you will be there.

I know
that when the waiting seems so long,
  you hear my prayer.

I know
that through the crash of falling worlds
  you're holding me.

I know
that life and death are yours
  eternally.

Mother Janet Stuart, 1857–1914

**In the morning,** in the evening,
God is holding you, holding you.
In the daytime, in the nighttime,
God is holding you still.

*Anywhere you may go,*
*God will go with you.*
*Anywhere you may go,*
*you are God's child.*

In the mountains, in the ocean,
God will carry you, carry you.
In the forest, in the cities,
God will carry you still.

*Anywhere you may go,*
*God will go with you.*
*Anywhere you may go,*
*you are God's child.*

In the good times, in the hard times,
God will stay with you, stay with you.
In your waking, in your sleeping,
God will stay with you still.

*Anywhere you may go,*
*God will go with you.*
*Anywhere you may go,*
*you are God's child.*

Adam M. L. Tice
© 2013, GIA Publications, Inc.
Meter: 8 8 8 6 6 5 6 4
*A musical setting of this hymn text is available, G-9873.*

**Peace,** be not anxious.
Our Maker is gracious.
Think now of the lilies: they toil not, nor spin.
Fields lush with adornment,
all Solomon's raiment,
still never could rival the splendor therein.

Fret not for tomorrow.
In joy or in sorrow,
each tiniest sparrow God will not forget.
Bright Spirit descending,
warm comfort unending—
peace, be not anxious: God cares for you yet.

Peace now I give to you.
My peace I pour through you.
Not as the world gives you, but ever more sure.
Past all understanding,
this gracious commanding:
peace, be not anxious. God holds you secure.

In mansions of heaven,
blest life will be given.
There, one with our Maker, I'll welcome you home.
Lo, I go before you.
So, now I implore you:
peace, be not anxious, for you are my own.

Mary Louise Bringle
*A musical setting of this hymn text is available, G-6710.*

**MY LORD GOD,** I have no idea where I am going. I do not see the road ahead of me. I cannot know for certain where it will end. Nor do I really know myself, and the fact that I think that I am following your will does not mean that I am actually doing so. But I believe that the desire to please you does in fact please you. And I hope I have that desire in all that I am doing. I hope that I will never do anything apart from that desire. And I know that if I do this you will lead me by the right road, though I may know nothing about it. Therefore will I trust you always, though I may seem to be lost and in the shadow of death. I will not fear, for you are ever with me, and you will never leave me to face my perils alone.

Thomas Merton, 1915–1968

## *Of* Womb *and* Tomb

**GOD SPEAKS** to each of us as he makes us,
then walks with us silently out of the night.

These are the words we dimly hear:

You, sent out beyond your recall,
go to the limits of your longing.
Embody me.

Flare up like a flame
and make big shadows I can move in.

Let everything happen to you: beauty and terror.
Just keep going. No feeling is final.
Don't let yourself lose me.

Nearby is the country they call life.
You will know it by its seriousness.

Give me your hand.

Rainer Maria Rilke, 1875–1926

Tr. Joanna Macy

*Rilke's Book of Hours: Love Poems to God*
© 1996, Anita Barrows and Joanna Macy

**HELD IN THE SHELTER** of God's wing,
terrors of night, we need not fear.
Our evening joys and cares we bring
as God inclines a listening ear.

Mother and midwife, cradling arms,
comfort when strength dries up like dust,
source of protection from life's harms:
we turn to you, our God, in trust.

None in your love are left alone.
Angels keep watch by those who sleep.
They who at night their tears have sown
by morning's light, in joy shall reap.

Mary Louise Bringle
© 2002, GIA Publications, Inc.
Meter: LM
*This hymn text may be sung to the tune of*
*"When Love Is Found" (O WALY WALY).*

*Blessing the Fragments*

CUP YOUR HANDS together,
and you will see the shape
this blessing wants to take.
Basket, bowl, vessel:
it cannot help but
hold itself open
to welcome
what comes.
This blessing
knows the secret
of the fragments
that find their way
into its keeping,
the wholeness
that may hide
in what has been
left behind,
the persistence of plenty
where there seemed
only lack.

Look into the hollows
of your hands
and ask
what wants to be
gathered there,
what abundance waits
among the scraps
that come to you,
what feast
will offer itself
from the fragments
that remain.

Jan Richardson
*The Cure for Sorrow:*
*A Book of Blessings for Times of Grief*
© 2016, Jan Richardson

# Of Womb and Tomb

**As tender** as a mother hen
who spreads her wings to shield her brood,
Christ Jesus stretches out his arms
and sheds his life as holy food.
> We seek his pattern in our hearts,
> amazed by such unselfish grace,
> and tend the children of the world
> in whom we see God's face.

Courageous as a mother bear
who guards her young from danger's path,
Christ Jesus wields his zealous love
and shows the gift of rightful wrath.
> We heed his call, opposing pow'rs
> that thwart the cause of life and health,
> and strive to reach the prophets' dreams
> to build God's Commonwealth.

A phoenix rising from the flames,
a mother eagle, soaring high,
Christ Jesus lifts the weary world
and conquers death for all who die.
> In him, we find our strength renewed
> and, mounting up on fledgling wings,
> we rise to share the gospel hope
> that resurrection brings!

Mary Louise Bringle

© 2006, GIA Publications, Inc.

Meter: 8 8 8 8 8 8 8 6

*This hymn text may be sung to the tune of*
*"Before the Marvel of This Night" (MARVEL).*

IN THE DARK before the dawning,
in the shadowed hours of loss,
in the depth of lonely sorrow,
God is hanging on the cross.

In the fall of ev'ry sparrow,
in the with'ring of each leaf,
in the smallest pains of passing,
God is with us in our grief.

In the silent ache of yearning,
in the silver of a tear,
in the stillest night of vigil,
God is whisp'ring: "I am here."

Mary Louise Bringle

© 2006, GIA Publications, Inc.
*This hymn text may be sung to the tune of*
*"Tree of Life" (THOMAS) by repeating*
*the final line of each stanza.*

*The Healing That Comes*

I KNOW how long
you have been waiting
for your story to take
a different turn,
how far
you have gone in search
of what will mend you
and make you whole.
I bear no remedy,
no cure,
no miracle
for the easing
of your pain.
But I know
the medicine
that lives in a story
that has been
broken open.

I know
the healing that comes
in ceasing
to hide ourselves away
with fingers clutched
around the fragments
we think are
none but ours.
See how they fit together,
these shards
we have been carrying—
how in their meeting
they make a way
we could not
find alone.

Jan Richardson
*The Cure for Sorrow:*
*A Book of Blessings for Times of Grief*
© 2016, Jan Richardson

**IN THE WAITING,**
Yes
In the grieving,
Yes
In the yearning,
Yes
In the questions,
Yes
In the anger,
Yes
In the openness,
Yes
In the doubt,
Yes
In your possibilities,
Yes
In your unexpected,
Yes
In your blessings,
Yes
In your vision,
Yes
In your mystery,
Yes
In your love,
Yes
In your will,
Yes

Let it be done to me.

Kate Williams
© 2019, GIA Publications, Inc.

**GIVER OF LIFE** and ev'ry good,
God beyond all we dare to dream,
hear now our prayer in Jesus' name;
praise be our never-ending theme.

Praise for foundations firm and strong;
praise for all faithful Christians past;
praise for the call that brought us here;
praise for the love that holds us fast.

Praise for the times of seed and flow'r,
fruit of the autumn, winter rest;
praise for the Spirit's work in all,
transforming love made manifest.

Praise for the grace that lies ahead,
comfort in hardship, strength in pain,
hunger for justice, thirst for peace,
till Christ in glory comes to reign.

God of our past and present years,
God of the future here begun,
guided by faith, we seek your face;
heartened by hope, we journey on.

Delores Dufner, OSB
© 2011, GIA Publications, Inc.
Meter: LM
*This hymn text may be sung to the tune of*
*"Take Up Your Cross" (BOURBON).*

**HOWEVER** long the night, the dawn will break.

African proverb

**THE SUN** wants to rise now
as though nothing terrible
happened in the night.

For the terrible thing
happened to me,
only me.
And the sun's light
shines on everyone.

Don't fold night inside you
Don't hold night inside you
Sink it down
not into darkness
but into light
Eternal
Forever.

A small light shining sweet in my tent
went out.

Great light, then, I greet you
Joyful light
World light

I greet you.

Jennifer K. Budziak

© 2018, Jennifer K. Budziak
Inspired by "Nun will die Sonn' so hell aufgeh'n"
by Friedrich Rückert, 1788–1866

**ALL WHO SEEK** to know and serve God,
see the past and understand:
none who hoped were disappointed;
rich the blessings from God's hand.
None who waited were forsaken;
none who trusted were deceived.
All who asked for gracious pardon,
gentle mercy have received.

If our God does not condemn us,
who against us then will stand?
Will the Lord, who died for sinners,
who is now at God's right hand?
What could take us from Christ Jesus?
Neither hunger, sword, nor pain.
Neither life nor death shall part us
from the Lamb for us once slain.

Let our hearts know peace in grieving;
joy awaits all those who mourn.
Christ has overcome the darkness;
death has died and life is born.
Let the empty tomb be witness:
our redeemer, Jesus, lives.
Let the cross be pledge of glory:
life forever Jesus gives.

Alleluia, alleluia,
joy awaits all those who mourn.
Alleluia, alleluia,
death has died and life is born.
Alleluia, alleluia,
our redeemer, Jesus, lives.
Alleluia, alleluia,
lasting glory Jesus gives!

Delores Dufner, OSB

Meter: 8 7 8 7 D
*This hymn text may be sung to the tune of*
*"God of Day and God of Darkness" (BEACH SPRING).*

LOOK AT HOW a single candle can both defy and define the darkness.

Anne Frank, 1929–1945

FOR THOSE WHO cannot find a way
 through bitter pain;
for those who cannot see a day
 they'll sing again;
  we pray, we weep, we cry,
  and why, O God? Why?

When nothing seems to heal the mind
 or calm our grief;
when chains of suff'ring choke and bind
 and test belief;
  we groan, we shake, we cry,
  and why, O God? Why?

Half-confident, we pray and shout
 through loss and fear;
we hope despite our honest doubt
 that God will hear
  our prayer, our song, our cry:
  our "Why, O God? Why?"

Adam M. L. Tice

Meter: 8 4 8 4 6 5
*A musical setting of this hymn text is available, G-9475.*

LORD, make me an instrument of your peace;
where there is hatred, let me sow love;
where there is injury, pardon;
where there is doubt, faith;
where there is despair, hope;
where there is darkness, light;
and where there is sadness, joy.

Attr. Francis of Assisi, 1182–1226

Poems, Hymns, and Blessings

**COME TO ME,** O weary traveler,
come to me with your distress,
come to me you heavy burdened,
come to me and find your rest.

*Do not fear, my yoke is easy,*
*do not fear, my burden's light;*
*do not fear the path before you;*
*do not run from me in fright.*

Take my yoke and leave your troubles;
take my yoke and come with me.
Take my yoke, I am beside you;
take and learn humility.

*Do not fear, my yoke is easy,*
*do not fear, my burden's light;*
*do not fear the path before you;*
*do not run from me in fright.*

Rest in me, O weary traveler,
rest in me and do not fear.
Rest in me, my heart is gentle,
rest and cast away your care.

*Do not fear, my yoke is easy,*
*do not fear, my burden's light;*
*do not fear the path before you;*
*do not run from me in fright.*

Sylvia G. Dunstan, 1955–1993

© 1991 GIA Publications, Inc.
Meter: 8 7 8 7 with Refrain
*A musical setting of this hymn text is available, G-9135.*

75

**THE BEST AND MOST** beautiful things in the world cannot be seen nor even touched, but just felt in the heart.

Helen Keller, 1880–1968

## Go down
into the plans of God.
Go down
deep as you may.
Fear not
for your fragility
under that weight of water.
Fear not
for life or limb
sharks attack savagely.
Fear not the power
of treacherous currents under the sea.
Simply, do not be afraid.
Let go. You will be led
like a child whose mother
holds him to her bosom
and against all comers is his shelter.

Dom Helder Camara, 1909–1999
*The Desert Is Fertile*
© 1974, Orbis Books

# *Of* WOMB *and* TOMB

THE GOD of Sarah praise,
the God of dreams long dead,
who births new life from barren ground,
disarming dread.
Though grief lasts through the night,
joy rises with the sun;
God leaves us laughing in surprise
at death undone.

The God of Abr'ham praise,
the God of all who roam,
who guides us into foreign lands
and makes our home.
Though darkness shrouds our path,
the stars, as pledges, shine;
God's covenant will be fullled
by love's design.

The God of Hagar praise,
the God of "second best"—
who sees the lost and overlooked
and calls them blessed.
Though wandering alone
through deserts of despair,
God leads us to a well of hope
and meets us there.

David Bjorlin

**Lord,**
I am tearing the heart of my soul in two.
I need you to come
and lie there yourself
in the wounds of my soul.

Mechtild of Magdeburg, ca. 1207–ca. 1282/1294

## Of Womb *and* Tomb

**SOMETIMES** our only song is weeping;
our only sound is gasping breath.
Sometimes it seems that God is sleeping
while our brief lives are bound in death.
Who hears the song our sorrows swallow
and offers hope to calm our fears?
When all our words seem frail and hollow,
God heeds the prayers within our tears.

Sometimes we catch the faintest humming,
a far-off tune our hearts know well.
Sometimes we sense the Spirit coming.
Our song returns; our voices swell.
The Spirit sings though we are shaken,
and Christ has shared our heart-felt cries.
Restored, our weary souls awaken
to join God's song that never dies.

Adam M. L. Tice
© 2015, GIA Publications, Inc.
Meter: 9 8 9 8 D
*This hymn text may be sung to the tune of
"Wayfaring Stranger."*

## St. Patrick's Breastplate

**I ARISE** today through
God's strength to pilot me, God's might to uphold me,
God's wisdom to guide me, God's eye to see before me,
God's ear to hear me, God's word to speak for me,
God's hand to guard me, God's way to lie before me,
God's shield to protect me, God's host to secure me—
against snares of devils,
against temptations and vices,
against inclinations of nature,
against everyone who shall wish me
ill, afar and anear,
alone and in a crowd...
Christ, be with me, Christ before me, Christ behind me,
Christ in me, Christ beneath me, Christ above me,
Christ on my right, Christ on my left, Christ where I lie,
    Christ where I sit,
Christ where I arise, Christ in the heart of every one
    who thinks of me,
Christ in the mouth of every one who speaks of me,
Christ in every eye that sees me, Christ in every ear that hears me.
Salvation is of the Lord.
Salvation is of the Lord.
Salvation is of the Christ.
May your salvation, O Lord, be ever with us.

Attr. St. Patrick, 5th c., tr. Anon.

**BE SURPRISED BY JOY,** be surprised by the little flower that shows its beauty in the midst of a barren desert, and be surprised by the immense healing power that keeps bursting forth like springs of fresh water from the depth of our pain.

Henri Nouwen, 1932–1996

**ONCE WE SANG** and danced with gladness,
Once delight filled ev'ry breath;
Now we sit among the ashes,
All our dreams destroyed by death.

All the willows bow in weeping,
All the rivers rage and moan
As creation joins our pleading:
"God, do not leave us alone."

God, who came to dwell among us,
God, who suffered our disgrace,
From your own heart, grieved and wounded,
Come the riches of your grace.

Come, O Christ, among these ashes,
Come to wipe our tears away,
Death destroy and sorrow banish;
Now and always, come and stay.

Susan Briehl

© 2003, GIA Publications, Inc.
Meter: 8 7 8 7
*A musical setting of this hymn text is available, G-6305.*

YOU WILL LOSE someone you can't live without, and your heart will be badly broken, and the bad news is that you never completely get over the loss of your beloved. But this is also the good news. They live forever in your broken heart that doesn't seal back up. And you come through. It's like having a broken leg that never heals perfectly—that still hurts when the weather gets cold, but you learn to dance with the limp.

Anne Lamott
© Anne Lamott

**AND HERE AM I,** budding
among the ruins
with only sorrow to bite on,
as if weeping were a seed and I
the earth's only furrow.

Pablo Neruda, 1904–1973
*Barrio Sin Luz (Lightless Suburb)*
Tr. Unknown

*On This Day: A Mother's Day Poem*

ON THIS DAY
when things have gone according to plan,
we don't think twice about today
Mother's Day is breakfast in bed
    flowers, tidy bouquets and wilty wildflowers
    messy kids' drawings—
        thank you to the teachers that reminded
    homemade coupons with no expiration
        for a 10-minute backrub
And this is good. holy.
And on this day
    when things have not gone according to plan,
    this day can be heartache embodied
Mother's Day is hiding in bed
    church blessing asking "moms" to come forward
        chalkboard brunch deals shouting your sorrow
            along your morning route
    deafening silence as you check your phone,
        again (no missed calls)
And this is hard. holy.

On this day—
    single aunties with aching wombs
    married women with aching wombs
    stepmoms who step in and step up
    grandmas raising Littles
    women who mother
    women with no longing to mother
    women who've miscarried

women who have buried their child, their children
women who are less valued in their family or society
    because you haven't birthed a human
women who've birthed humans with their body
women who've birthed humans through adoptive love
mothers who are tired of mom shaming
mothers struggling to put food on the table
mothers who visit their kid behind bars
mothers who feel they have failed
mothers who work outside the home
mothers who stay at home and work—

You are seen. You are good. holy.
    Life is hard. holy.
    Whole and broken.
    Utterly heartbreaking and ordinary
        and weak-at-knees beautiful all at once
    On this day, let it be true, all of it. Any of it.
On this day, let it be known,
    whether your tears are rooted in joy, longing, frustration,
    or the heartbreak associated with being a woman,
    a mother, on this day,
let it be known—
    You are good. holy. beloved.

Melissa Carnall

# PRAYERS *for the* CHILD

**GOD OUR CREATOR,**
you called into being this fragile life,
which had seemed to us so full of promise.
Give to *N.,* whom we commit to your care,
abundant life in your presence,
and to us who grieve,
courage to bear our loss;
through Jesus Christ our Lord and Savior.

*Evangelical Lutheran Worship Pastoral Care*

**O GOD,** whose beloved Son took children into his arms
    and blessed them:
Give us grace to entrust *N.* to your never-failing care and love,
and bring us all to your heavenly kingdom;
through Jesus Christ our Lord,
who lives and reigns with you and the Holy Spirit,
one God forever and ever. Amen.

*The Book of Common Prayer*

**MERCIFUL GOD,** your Spirit intercedes for us
even when we do not know how to pray.
Be present among us now,
that we might commend ***N.*** / *this child* / *this pregnancy*
into your loving care and, by your presence,
find comfort; through Jesus Christ, your Son, our Savior.

*Evangelical Lutheran Worship Pastoral Care*

**TO YOU,** O Lord,
we humbly entrust this child
so precious in your sight.
Take *him/her* into your arms
and welcome *him/her* into paradise
where there will be no sorrow, no weeping nor pain,
but the fullness of peace and joy
with your Son and the Holy Spirit
for ever and ever. Amen.

*Order of Christian Funerals*

**WE GIVE BACK TO YOU,** O God,
those whom you gave to us.
You did not lose them when you gave them to us,
and we do not lose them by their return to you.
Your dear Son has taught us
that life is eternal
and love cannot die.
So death is only a horizon
and a horizon is only the limit of our sight.
Open our eyes to see more clearly,
and draw us closer to you
that we may know that we are nearer to our loved ones,
who are with you.
You have told us that you are preparing a place for us;
prepare us also for that happy place,
that where you are we may also be always,
O dear Lord of life and death.

William Penn, 1644–1718

**O GOD,**
your love cares for us in life
and watches over us in death.
We bless you for our Savior's joy in little children
and for the assurance that of such is the kingdom of heaven.
In our sorrow,
make us strong to commit ourselves, and those we love,
to your unfailing care.
In our perplexity,
help us to trust where we cannot understand.
In our loneliness,
may we remember *N.* in love,
trusting *him/her* to your keeping
until the eternal morning breaks,
through Jesus Christ our Lord. Amen.

*Book of Common Worship*

MAY GOD REMEMBER my *daughter N. bat [parents] N. and N. / son N. ben [parents] N. and N.,* who has gone to eternal rest. *Her/His* life was but the briefest flicker of a flame, extinguished before it had time to shed its light on the world but not before sharing its warmth with me.

Through the months of *her/his* gestation, I prepared to nurture and to love *her/him.* For the time that *she/he* lived, I gave to *her/him* everything a parent could have given and received everything I could have expected.

May the memory of the joy *she/he* brought to me in the short time that we were together strengthen me, and may God count that joy as the weight of a life filled with such blessing, binding through that love and joy **N. bat/ben [parents] N. and N.** in the bonds of eternal life.

For the gift of *her/his* life without transgression, I pledge to do acts of righteousness and *tzedakah** that *she/he* may merit eternal life and that I may find comfort in this world.

Rabbi Ira F. Stone
© *Ira F. Stone*

---

**charity*

## LORD GOD,

ever caring and gentle,
we commit to your love this little one,
quickened to life for so short a time.
Enfold *him/her* in eternal life.
We pray for *his/her* parents
who are saddened by the loss of their child.
Give them courage
and help them in their grief and pain.
May they all meet one day
in the joy and the peace of your kingdom.
We ask this through Christ our Lord.

*Order of Christian Funerals*

**HEAVENLY FATHER,**
your love for all children is strong and enduring.
We were not able to know *this child / N.*
as we hoped.
Yet you knew *her/him* growing in *her/his* mother's womb,
and *she/he* is not lost to you.
In the midst of our sadness,
we thank you that *this child / N.*
is with you now, and with you forever.

*Evangelical Lutheran Worship Pastoral Care*

**LOVING GOD,**
give us faith to believe
though this child has died,
that you welcome *him/her*
and will care for *him/her*
until, by your mercy,
we are together again in the joy of your promised kingdom;
through Jesus Christ our Lord. Amen.

*Book of Common Worship*

**JESUS SAID,** "Let the children come to me.
   Do not keep them from me.
The kingdom of God belongs to such as these."
Eternal rest grant unto *him/her*, O Lord.
   *R/.* And let perpetual light shine upon him/her.
May *he/she* rest in peace.
   *R/.* Amen.
May *his/her* soul and the souls of all the faithful departed,
through the mercy of God, rest in peace.

*Order of Christian Funerals*

**IN THE RISING** of the sun and in its going down,
we remember them.
In the beginning of the year and when it ends,
we remember them.
When we are weary and in need of strength
we remember them.
When we are lost and sick at heart,
we remember them.
So long as we live,
they too shall live,
for they are now a part of us,
as we remember them.

Jewish prayer for a holy day

**Into your gentle keeping,** O Lord,
we commend this child, *N.*
Though our hearts are troubled
we hope in your loving kindness.
May the angels, our guardians,
lead *N.* now to paradise
where your saints will welcome *him/her*
and every tear shall be wiped away.
There we shall join in songs of praise for ever.
We ask this through Christ our Lord. Amen.

*Order of Christian Funerals*

**N., CHILD OF GOD,**
we entrust you to the arms of God's mercy.
Almighty God, who formed us all out of the dust of the earth,
receive you in peace.
Christ the Good Shepherd, enfold you in his tender care.
God the Holy Spirit, our Comforter,
bear you to life in God's new creation.
May you dwell forever in the paradise of God. Amen.

*Evangelical Lutheran Worship Pastoral Care*

# Prayers *of/for the* Parents *and* Those Who Mourn

O GOD, who gathered Rachel's tears over her lost children,
hear now the sorrow and distress of *N.* and *N.*,
for the death of *her/their* expected child.
In the darkness of loss, stretch out to *her/them*
the strength of your arm and renewed assurance of your love;
through your own suffering and risen Son, Jesus our Savior.

*Evangelical Lutheran Worship Pastoral Care*

**I TOOK CARE** of myself, God.
I made sure to eat right, and tried to do a few less dishes.
I told the doctors about all of my aches and pains, just to be sure.
Just to be sure that the baby was okay.
Everything was fine if the baby was fine.

I was getting closer to my baby.
She and I would do lots of things together.
And sometimes she'd even try to get my attention
     while I was working!
That way, I knew the baby was fine.

And now this.
Now things aren't fine.
Haven't I suffered enough loss?
Why did this happen to me?
Why did this happen to us?

She was so beautiful, God.
She was so dear.
She was ours.
I got to hold her.
And now I have to let go.

I was supposed to give thanks at this time.
But I feel empty inside.
Give me the space I need to mourn this loss.
A loss that is so hard to explain, so hard to comprehend.

Give my body time to rest, God.
Let my body begin to heal, as it has undergone such trauma.
Allow me to take the time I need to regain my energy.

Give *N.* and me the strength we need to get through this.
Continue to allow my *spouse / partner / friends* to be there for me,
as *he/she has / they have* always been.
When I am ready, let my friends bring me comfort.
So I can smile once again.

I did everything I could, God.
I was a good carrier!
Life was granted inside of me, and now it has been removed.

Please provide *N.* and I with love and comfort
    as we face this reality.
Protect us as we grapple with this loss.
Support us as we continue to look toward building a family.

Barukh Atah Adoshem, Rofeh Holim.
    Blessed are You, God, who heals.

Rabbi Yael Buechler
© 2009, Rabbi Yael Buechler

*Of* WOMB *and* TOMB

**O GOD** of the Waiting,
We are Abraham and Sarah,
    no longer sure what it means to trust in your promise
We are your people wandering in the desert,
    certain that 40 years is too long to bear
We are the woman hemorrhaging for 12 years,
    desperate to touch your cloak
You are our only hope
We long to bear a child,
    to create and love as You create and love us
    to teach our child they are your child, a child of God
We place our longing in your hands,
    Knowing that faith is the opposite of certainty
    Trusting You will be with us wherever this waiting leads
    Trusting there will be new life after our sorrow,
    water in our desert wandering,
      and response to our despairing pleas
Asking all this in the name of the One
    who constantly waits for us with open arms,
    our Savior, Jesus Christ,
Amen.

Melissa Carnall

*After Miscarriage or Stillbirth*

## SOURCE AND SHIELD,

You have made my body
To be a fountain of life,
A well of strength,
To take seed into the warmth of my womb,
To feed and hold,
To love and shelter,
To awaken new life.
Oh grief,
I am stripped bare,
The cradle of my body empty,
My heart bereft.
Oh sorrow,
My soul yearns, aches, weeps
For the one who will never rest in my arms.
Oh God,
Witness my distress,
My suffering and loss.
When will the days bring comfort and rest?
When will the nights bring solace and peace?
Hear my prayer.
Lead me on a path,
God of our mothers,
God of generations,
A path that now seems so distant, so remote,
A path of wholeness and healing.

Alden Solovy
*Jewish Prayers of Hope and Healing*

**OUT OF THE DEPTHS** we cry to you, O loving God.
Come near to those whose hearts are torn with grief and sorrow,
for you know and share our tears.
Help us to trust your care,
so that even in the pain of losing this little one / *N.*
we may be assured that we do not walk alone
in the valley of death;
through Jesus Christ our Savior and Lord.

*Evangelical Lutheran Worship Pastoral Care*

## Lord Jesus,

whose Mother stood grieving at the foot of the cross,
look kindly on these parents
who have suffered the loss of their child *N.*
Listen to the prayers of Mary on their behalf,
that their faith may be strong like hers
and find its promised reward,
for you live for ever and ever. Amen.

*Order of Christian Funerals*

*Loss of Pregnancy (men/partners)*

## GOD OF OLD,
What can I say before You?
I am crushed,
Flattened by sadness,
Cut down by grief.
Yet my *wife/partner/spouse* needs
My courage and my tears,
My gentleness and my strength.
Our lives,
Once ripe with promise,
Feel vacant and hollow,
And I have touched
A new loneliness and despair.
Rock of Ages,
Why have You raised our hopes only to take them away?
Why have you abandoned our prayers and our dreams?
What comfort remains?

Source and Shelter,
Teach me to honor, to balance and to express
Both my pain and my fortitude,
My endurance and my sorrow,
In service to You,
In service to my *wife/partner/spouse*,
In service to myself.
Lead *me/us* out of this darkness,
Back to awe and wonder,
So *I/we* may know,
Once again,
Hope and joy,
Gratitude and peace.

Alden Solovy

**MOST MERCIFUL GOD,**
whose wisdom is beyond our understanding:
Deal graciously with *N.* and *N.* in their grief.
Surround them with your love,
that they may not be overwhelmed by their loss,
but have confidence in your goodness,
and strength to meet the days to come;
through Jesus Christ our Lord. Amen

*The Book of Common Prayer*

## GOD OF ALL HOPE,

You know how this couple has hoped for this child,
    how they had begun to have specific hopes
    and dreams for their little one.
We don't understand, God, why
    why they won't get to see their little one born
        and grow and thrive
And so we do the only thing we can—
We lift our hearts to You, O God,
the One who never leaves us alone in our suffering
Let *N.* and *N.* know
    how You are with them now in their sorrow.
    Comfort them in their weeping.
    Hold their hearts as they seek to hold their hope in You,
In the name of Jesus, our God-with-us
Amen.

Melissa Carnall

**HOLY GOD,**
yours is the beauty of childhood
and yours is the fullness of years.
Comfort us in our sorrow,
strengthen us with hope,
and breathe peace into our troubled hearts.
Assure us that the love in which we rejoiced for a time
is not lost,
and that *N.* is with you,
safe in your eternal love and care.
We ask this in the name of Jesus Christ,
who took little children in his arms and blessed them. Amen.

*Book of Common Worship*

**God of all consolation,**
searcher of mind and heart,
the faith of these parents *N.* and *N.* is known to you.
Comfort them with the knowledge
that the child for whom they grieve
is entrusted now to your loving care.
We ask this through Christ our Lord. Amen.

*Order of Christian Funerals*

**YOU ARE THE AUTHOR** and sustainer of our lives, O God,
you are our final home.
We commend to you *N.*, our child.
Trusting in your mercy
and in your all-embracing love,
we pray that you give *him/her* happiness for ever.
Turn also to us who have suffered this loss.
Strengthen the bonds of this family and our community.
Confirm us in faith, in hope, and in love,
so that we may bear your peace to one another
and one day stand together with all the saints
who praise you for your saving help.
We ask this in the name of your Son,
Jesus Christ our Lord. Amen.

*Order of Christian Funerals*

# SCRIPTURES

**PEOPLE WERE BRINGING** little children to Jesus in order that he might touch them; and the disciples spoke sternly to them. But when Jesus saw this, he was indignant and said to them, "Let the little children come to me; do not stop them; for it is to such as these that the kingdom of God belongs. Truly I tell you, whoever does not receive the kingdom of God as a little child will never enter it." And he took them up in his arms, laid his hands on them, and blessed them.

Mark 10:13–16

AT THAT TIME JESUS SAID, "I thank you, Father, Lord of heaven and earth, because you have hidden these things from the wise and the intelligent and have revealed them to infants; yes, Father, for such was your gracious will. All things have been handed over to me by my Father; and no one knows the Son except the Father, and no one knows the Father except the Son and anyone to whom the Son chooses to reveal him. Come to me, all you that are weary and are carrying heavy burdens, and I will give you rest. Take my yoke upon you, and learn from me; for I am gentle and humble in heart, and you will find rest for your souls."

Matthew 11:25–29

**THEN LITTLE CHILDREN** were being brought to him in order that he might lay his hands on them and pray. The disciples spoke sternly to those who brought them; but Jesus said, "Let the little children come to me, and do not stop them; for it is to such as these that the kingdom of heaven belongs." And he laid his hands on them and went on his way.

Matthew 19:13–15

**PEOPLE WERE BRINGING** even infants to him that he might touch them; and when the disciples saw it, they sternly ordered them not to do it. But Jesus called for them and said, "Let the little children come to me, and do not stop them; for it is to such as these that the kingdom of God belongs. Truly I tell you, whoever does not receive the kingdom of God as a little child will never enter it."

Luke 18:15–17

**JESUS SAID TO THE CROWD:** "Everything that the Father gives me will come to me, and anyone who comes to me I will never drive away; for I have come down from heaven, not to do my own will, but the will of him who sent me. And this is the will of him who sent me, that I should lose nothing of all that he has given me, but raise it up on the last day. This is indeed the will of my Father, that all who see the Son and believe in him may have eternal life; and I will raise them up on the last day."

John 6:37–40

**STANDING NEAR THE CROSS** of Jesus were his mother, and his mother's sister, Mary the wife of Clopas, and Mary Magdalene. When Jesus saw his mother and the disciple whom he loved standing beside her, he said to his mother, "Woman, here is your son." Then he said to the disciple, "Here is your mother." And from that hour the disciple took her into his own home. After this, when Jesus knew that all was now finished, he said (in order to fulfill the scripture), "I am thirsty." A jar full of sour wine was standing there. So they put a sponge full of the wine on a branch of hyssop and held it to his mouth. When Jesus had received the wine, he said, "It is finished." Then he bowed his head and gave up his spirit.

John 19:25–30

JESUS SAID, "I am the good shepherd. The good shepherd lays down his life for the sheep. The hired hand, who is not the shepherd and does not own the sheep, sees the wolf coming and leaves the sheep and runs away—and the wolf snatches them and scatters them. The hired hand runs away because a hired hand does not care for the sheep. I am the good shepherd. I know my own and my own know me, just as the Father knows me and I know the Father. And I lay down my life for the sheep."

John 10:11–16

**THE STEADFAST LOVE** of the Lord never ceases, his mercies never come to an end; they are new every morning; great is your faithfulness. "The Lord is my portion," says my soul, "therefore I will hope in him." The Lord is good to those who wait for him, to the soul that seeks him. It is good that one should wait quietly for the salvation of the Lord.

Lamentations 3:22–26

**THUS SAYS THE LORD:** A voice is heard in Ramah, lamentation and bitter weeping. Rachel is weeping for her children; she refuses to be comforted for her children, because they are no more. Thus says the Lord: Keep your voice from weeping, and your eyes from tears; for there is a reward for your work, says the Lord: they shall come back from the land of the enemy; there is hope for your future, says the Lord: your children shall come back to their own country.

Jeremiah 31:15–17

**THUS SAYS THE LORD,**
    he who created you, O Jacob,
    he who formed you, O Israel:
Do not fear, for I have redeemed you;
    I have called you by name, you are mine.
When you pass through the waters, I will be with you;
    and through the rivers, they shall not overwhelm you;
when you walk through fire you shall not be burned,
    and the flame shall not consume you.
For I am the Lord your God,
    the Holy One of Israel, your Savior.

Isaiah 43:1–3

**LISTEN TO ME,** O coastlands, pay attention, you peoples from far away! "The Lord called me before I was born, while I was in my mother's womb he named me." Can a woman forget her nursing child, or show no compassion for the child of her womb? Even these may forget, yet I will not forget you. See, I have inscribed you on the palms of my hands; your walls are continually before me.

Isaiah 49:1, 15–16

**THUS SAYS THE LORD:** I will return to Zion, and will dwell in the midst of Jerusalem; Jerusalem shall be called the faithful city, and the mountain of the Lord of hosts shall be called the holy mountain. Thus says the Lord of hosts: Old men and old women shall again sit in the streets of Jerusalem, each with staff in hand because of their great age. And the streets of the city shall be full of boys and girls playing in its streets. Thus says the Lord of hosts: Even though it seems impossible to the remnant of this people in these days, should it also seem impossible to me, says the Lord of hosts? Thus says the Lord of hosts: I will save my people from the east country and from the west country; and I will bring them to live in Jerusalem. They shall be my people and I will be their God, in faithfulness and in righteousness.

Zechariah 8:1–8

**SEE WHAT LOVE** the Father has given us, that we should be called children of God; and that is what we are. The reason the world does not know us is that it did not know him. Beloved, we are God's children now; what we will be has not yet been revealed. What we do know is this: when he is revealed, we will be like him, for we will see him as he is.

1 John 3:1–2

CHRIST HAS BEEN RAISED from the dead, the first fruits of those who have died. For since death came through a human being, the resurrection of the dead has also come through a human being; for as all die in Adam, so all will be made alive in Christ. But each in his own order: Christ the first fruits, then at his coming those who belong to Christ.

1 Corinthians 15:20–23

**BLESSED BE THE GOD** and Father of our Lord Jesus Christ, who has blessed us in Christ with every spiritual blessing in the heavenly places, just as he chose us in Christ before the foundation of the world to be holy and blameless before him in love. He destined us for adoption as his children through Jesus Christ.

Ephesians 1:3–5

**WE DO NOT WANT YOU TO BE UNINFORMED,** brothers and sisters, about those who have died, so that you may not grieve as others do who have no hope. For since we believe that Jesus died and rose again, even so, through Jesus, God will bring with him those who have died. For this we declare to you by the word of the Lord, that we who are alive, who are left until the coming of the Lord, will by no means precede those who have died. For the Lord himself, with a cry of command, with the archangel's call and with the sound of God's trumpet, will descend from heaven, and the dead in Christ will rise first. Then we who are alive, who are left, will be caught up in the clouds together with them to meet the Lord in the air; and so we will be with the Lord forever. Therefore encourage one another with these words.

1 Thessalonians 4:13–18

AFTER THIS I LOOKED, and there was a great multitude that no one could count, from every nation, from all tribes and peoples and languages, standing before the throne and before the Lamb, robed in white, with palm branches in their hands. They cried out in a loud voice, saying, "Salvation belongs to our God who is seated on the throne, and to the Lamb!" And all the angels stood around the throne and around the elders and the four living creatures, and they fell on their faces before the throne and worshiped God, singing, "Amen! Blessing and glory and wisdom and thanksgiving and honor and power and might be to our God forever and ever! Amen." Then one of the elders addressed me, saying, "Who are these, robed in white, and where have they come from?" I said to him, "Sir, you are the one that knows." Then he said to me, "These are they who have come out of the great ordeal; they have washed their robes and made them white in the blood of the Lamb. For this reason they are before the throne of God, and worship him day and night within his temple, and the one who is seated on the throne will shelter them. They will hunger no more, and thirst no more; the sun will not strike them, nor any scorching heat; for the Lamb at the center of the throne will be their shepherd, and he will guide them to springs of the water of life, and God will wipe away every tear from their eyes."

Revelation 7:9–17

**THEN I SAW A NEW HEAVEN** and a new earth; for the first heaven and the first earth had passed away, and the sea was no more. And I saw the holy city, the new Jerusalem, coming down out of heaven from God, prepared as a bride adorned for her husband. And I heard a loud voice from the throne saying, "See, the home of God is among mortals. He will dwell with them as their God; they will be his peoples, and God himself will be with them; he will wipe every tear from their eyes. Death will be no more; mourning and crying and pain will be no more, for the first things have passed away." And the one who was seated on the throne said, "See, I am making all things new."

Revelation 21:1–5a

# PSALMODY

# Psalm 23

*Response:* **The Lord is my shepherd; there is nothing I shall want.**

The LORD is my shepherd;
there is nothing I shall want.
Fresh and green are the pastures
where he gives me repose.
Near restful waters he leads me;
he revives my soul. **R/.**

He guides me along the right path,
for the sake of his name.
Though I should walk
    in the valley of the shadow of death,
no evil would I fear, for you are with me.
Your crook and your staff will give me comfort. **R/.**

You have prepared a table before me
in the sight of my foes.
My head you have anointed with oil;
my cup is overflowing. **R/.**

Surely goodness and mercy shall follow me
all the days of my life.
In the LORD's own house shall I dwell
for length of days unending. **R/.**

## PSALM 25
*Verses 6, 7b, 17–18, 20–21*

*Response:* **To you, O Lord, I lift my soul.**
or:
*Response:* **No one who waits for you, O Lord,
   will ever be put to shame.**

Remember your compassion, O LORD,
and your merciful love,
for they are from of old.
In your merciful love remember me,
because of your goodness, O LORD. *R/.*

Relieve the anguish of my heart,
and set me free from my distress.
See my lowliness and suffering,
and take away all my sins. *R/.*

Preserve my life and rescue me.
Let me not be put to shame,
for in you I trust.
May integrity and virtue protect me,
for I have hoped in you, O LORD. *R/.*

# PSALM 27
*Verses 1, 4–5, 7–10, 13–14*

*Response:* **The Lord is my light and my salvation.**
or:
*Response:* **I believe that I shall see the good things of the Lord in the land of the living.**

The LORD is my light and my salvation;
whom shall I fear?
The LORD is the stronghold of my life;
whom should I dread? *R/.*

There is one thing I ask of the LORD,
only this do I seek:
to live in the house of the LORD
all the days of my life,
to gaze on the beauty of the LORD,
to inquire at his temple. *R/.*

For there he keeps me safe in his shelter
in the day of evil.
He hides me under cover of his tent;
he sets me high upon a rock. *R/.*

O LORD, hear my voice when I call;
have mercy and answer me.
Of you my heart has spoken,
"Seek his face." *R/.*

It is your face, O LORD, that I seek;
hide not your face from me.
Dismiss not your servant in anger;
you have been my help. *R/.*

Do not abandon or forsake me,
O God, my Savior!
Though father and mother forsake me,
the LORD will receive me. *R/.*

I believe I shall see the LORD's goodness
in the land of the living.
Wait for the LORD; be strong;
be stouthearted, and wait for the LORD! *R/.*

# Psalm 42

*Verses 2–6, 8–12*

*Response:* **My soul is thirsting for the living God:**
   **when shall I see him face to face?**

Like the deer that yearns
for running streams,
so my soul is yearning
for you, my God. **R/.**

My soul is thirsting for God,
the living God;
when can I enter and appear
before the face of God? **R/.**

My tears have become my bread,
by day, by night,
as they say to me all the day long,
"Where is your God?" **R/.**

These things will I remember
as I pour out my soul:
for I would go to the place
of your wondrous tent,
all the way to the house of God,
amid cries of gladness and thanksgiving,
the throng keeping joyful festival. **R/.**

## Of Womb *and* Tomb

Why are you cast down, my soul;
why groan within me?
Hope in God; I will praise him yet again,
my saving presence and my God. *R/.*

Deep is calling on deep,
in the roar of your torrents;
your billows and all your waves
swept over me. *R/.*

By day the LORD decrees
his merciful love;
by night his song is with me,
prayer to the God of my life. *R/.*

I will say to God, my rock,
"Why have you forgotten me?
Why do I go mourning
oppressed by the foe?" *R/.*

With a deadly wound in my bones,
my enemies revile me,
saying to me all the day long,
"Where is your God?" *R/.*

Why are you cast down, my soul;
why groan within me?
Hope in God; I will praise him yet again,
my saving presence and my God. *R/.*

# PSALM 63
*Verses 2–6, 8–9*

*Response:* **My soul is thirsting for you, O Lord my God.**

O God, you are my God; at dawn I seek you;
for you my soul is thirsting.
For you my flesh is pining,
like a dry, weary land without water. **R/.**

I have come before you in the sanctuary,
to behold your strength and your glory.
Your loving mercy is better than life;
my lips will speak your praise. **R/.**

I will bless you all my life;
in your name I will lift up my hands.
My soul shall be filled as with a banquet;
with joyful lips, my mouth shall praise you. **R/.**

For you have been my strength;
in the shadow of your wings I rejoice.
My soul clings fast to you;
your right hand upholds me. **R/.**

## PSALM 88

*Response:* **Let my prayer come into your presence.**
 **Incline your ear to my cry.**

O LORD and God of my salvation,
I cry before you day and night.
Let my prayer come into your presence.
Incline your ear to my cry. *R/.*

For my soul is filled with evils;
my life is on the brink of the grave.
I am reckoned as one in the tomb;
I am like a warrior without strength,
like one roaming among the dead,
like the slain lying in their graves,
like those you remember no more,
cut off, as they are, from your hand. *R/.*

You have laid me in the depths of the pit,
in regions that are dark and deep.
Your anger weighs down upon me;
I am drowned beneath your waves. *R/.*

You have taken away my friends;
to them you have made me hateful.
Imprisoned, I cannot escape;
my eyes are sunken with grief.
I call to you, LORD, all day long;
to you I stretch out my hands. *R/.*

# Psalmody

Will you work your wonders for the dead?
Will the shades rise up to praise you?
Will your mercy be told in the grave,
or your faithfulness in the place of perdition?
Will your wonders be known in the dark,
your justice in the land of oblivion? *R/.*

But I, O LORD, cry out to you;
in the morning my prayer comes before you.
Why do you reject me, O LORD?
Why do you hide your face from me? *R/.*

I am wretched, close to death from my youth.
I have borne your trials; I am numb.
Your fury has swept down upon me;
your terrors have utterly destroyed me. *R/.*

They surround me all the day like a flood;
together they close in against me.
Friend and neighbor you have taken away:
my one companion is darkness. *R/.*

# PSALM 103
*Verses 8, 10, 13–18*

*Response:* ***The Lord is kind and merciful.***
or:
*Response:* ***The salvation of the just comes from the Lord.***

The LORD is compassionate and gracious,
slow to anger and rich in mercy.
He does not treat us according to our sins,
nor repay us according to our faults. *R/.*

As a father has compassion on his children,
the LORD's compassion is on those who fear him.
For he knows of what we are made;
he remembers that we are dust. *R/.*

Man, his days are like grass;
he flowers like the flower of the field.
The wind blows, and it is no more,
and its place never sees it again. *R/.*

But the mercy of the LORD is everlasting
upon those who hold him in fear,
upon children's children his justice,
for those who keep his covenant,
and remember to fulfill his commands. *R/.*

# PSALM 116
*Verses 5–6, 10–13, 15–16ac*

*Response:* **I will walk in the presence of the Lord
in the land of the living.**
or, if it is not Lent:
*Response:* **Alleluia!**

How gracious is the LORD, and just;
our God has compassion.
The LORD protects the simple;
I was brought low, and he saved me. **R/.**

I trusted, even when I said,
"I am sorely afflicted,"
and when I said in my alarm,
"These people are all liars." **R/.**

How can I repay the LORD
for all his goodness to me?
The cup of salvation I will raise;
I will call on the name of the LORD. **R/.**

How precious in the eyes of the LORD
is the death of his faithful.
Your servant, LORD, your servant am I,
you have loosened my bonds. **R/.**

## Psalm 130

*Response:* **Out of the depths I cry to you, O Lord.**
or:
*Response:* **I hope in the Lord, I trust in his word.**

Out of the depths I cry to you, O LORD;
Lord, hear my voice!
O let your ears be attentive
to the sound of my pleadings. *R/.*

If you, O LORD, should mark iniquities,
Lord, who could stand?
But with you is found forgiveness,
that you may be revered. *R/.*

I long for you, O LORD,
my soul longs for his word.
My soul hopes in the Lord
more than watchmen for daybreak. *R/.*

More than watchmen for daybreak,
let Israel hope for the LORD.
For with the LORD there is mercy,
in him is plentiful redemption. *R/.*

It is he who will redeem Israel
from all its iniquities. *R/.*

# PSALM 131

*Response:* **In you, O Lord, I have found my peace.**

O LORD, my heart is not proud,
nor haughty my eyes.
I have not gone after things too great,
nor marvels beyond me. *R/.*

Truly, I have set my soul
in tranquility and silence.
As a weaned child on its mother,
as a weaned child is my soul within me. *R/.*

O Israel, wait for the LORD,
both now and forever. *R/.*

## PSALM 138

*Response:* **In the sight of the angels, I will sing your praises, Lord.**

I thank you, LORD, with all my heart;
you have heard the words of my mouth.
In the presence of the angels I praise you.
I bow down toward your holy temple. *R/.*

I give thanks to your name
for your merciful love and your faithfulness.
You have exalted your name over all.
On the day I called, you answered me;
you increased the strength of my soul. *R/.*

All earth's kings shall thank you, O LORD,
when they hear the words of your mouth.
They shall sing of the ways of the LORD,
"How great is the glory of the LORD!" *R/.*

The LORD is high, yet he looks on the lowly,
and the haughty he knows from afar.
You give me life though I walk amid affliction;
you stretch out your hand
     against the anger of my foes. *R/.*

With your right hand you save me;
the LORD will accomplish this for me.
O LORD, your merciful love is eternal;
discard not the work of your hands. *R/.*

# PSALM 143
*Verses 1–2, 5–7ab, 8ab, 10*

*Response:* **O Lord, hear my prayer.**

O LORD, listen to my prayer;
turn your ear to my appeal.
You are faithful, you are just; give answer.
Do not call your servant to judgment,
for in your sight no one living is justified. *R/.*

I remember the days that are past;
I ponder all your works.
I muse on what your hand has wrought,
and to you I stretch out my hands.
Like a parched land my soul thirsts for you. *R/.*

O Lord, make haste and answer me,
for my spirit fails within me.
In the morning, let me know your loving mercy,
for in you I place my trust. *R/.*

Teach me to do your will,
for you are my God.
Let your good spirit guide me
upon ground that is level. *R/.*

# RITES *and* RITUALS

# BLESSING *of* PARENTS
## *after a* MISCARRIAGE

In times of death and grief the Christian turns to the Lord for consolation and strength. This is especially true when a child dies before birth. This blessing is provided to assist the parents in their grief and console them with the blessing of God.

These orders may be used by a priest or a deacon, and also by a layperson, who follows the rights and prayers designated for a lay minister.

## Introductory Rites

*The leader says:*

> In the name of the Father, and of the Son, and of the Holy Spirit.

*All make the sign of the cross and reply:*

> *R/.* Amen.

*The leader begins:*

> Let us praise the Father of mercies,
> the God of all consolation.
> Blessed be God for ever.
>
> *R/.* Blessed be God for ever.

*In the following or similar words, the leader prepares those present for the blessing.*

> For those who trust in God,
> in the pain of sorrow there is consolation,
> in the face of despair there is hope,
> in the midst of death there is life.
> **N.** and **N.**, as we mourn the death of your child,
> we place ourselves in the hands of God
> and ask for strength, for healing, and for love.

## Reading of the Word of God

*One of those present or the leader reads a text of sacred Scripture (Lamentations 3:17–26).*

> Brothers and sisters, listen to the words of the book of Lamentations:

> My soul is deprived of peace,
> I have forgotten what happiness is;
> I tell myself my future is lost,
> all that I hoped for from the Lord.
> The thought of my homeless poverty
> is wormwood and gall;
> Remembering it over and over
> leaves my soul downcast within me.
> But I will call this to mind,
> as my reason to have hope:
> The favors of the LORD are not exhausted,
> his mercies are not spent;
> They are renewed each morning,
> so great is his faithfulness.

My portion is the LORD, says my soul;
therefore will I hope in him.
Good is the LORD to one who waits for him,
to the soul that seeks him;
It is good to hope in silence
for the saving help of the LORD.

*Or:*

Isaiah 49:8–13
> *In a time of favor I answer you, on the day of salvation
> I help you.*

Romans 8:18–27
> *In hope we were saved.*

Romans 8:26–31
> *If God is for us, who can be against us?*

Colossians 1:9–12
> *We have been praying for you unceasingly.*

*As circumstances suggest, the following responsorial psalm may be sung, or some other suitable song.*

**R/.** To you, O Lord, I lift up my soul.

Your ways, O LORD, make known to me;
teach me your paths,
Guide me in your truth and teach me,
for you are God my savior,
and for you I wait all the day. **R/.**

Remember that your compassion, O LORD,
and your kindness are from of old.
The sins of my youth
    and my frailties remember not;
in your kindness remember me
because of your goodness, O LORD. *R/.*

Look toward me, and have pity on me,
for I am alone and afflicted.
Relieve the troubles of my heart,
and bring me out of my distress. *R/.*

Preserve my life, and rescue me;
let me not be put to shame,
    for I take refuge in you.
Let integrity and uprightness preserve me,
because I wait for you, O LORD. *R/.*

*As circumstances suggest, the leader may give those present a brief explanation of the biblical text, so that they may understand through faith the meaning of the celebration.*

**Intercessions**

*The intercessions are then said.*

Let us pray to God who throughout the ages has heard the cries of parents.

*R/.* Lord, hear our prayer.

For *N.* and *N.*, who know the pain of grief, that they may be comforted, we pray. *R/.*

For this family, that it may find new hope in the midst of suffering, we pray. *R/.*

For these parents, that they may learn from the example of Mary, who grieved by the cross of her Son, we pray. *R/.*

For all who have suffered the loss of a child, that Christ may be their support, we pray. *R/.*

*After the intercessions, the leader invites all to say the Lord's Prayer.*

## Prayer of Blessing

*The leader says the prayer of blessing with hands joined.*

> Compassionate God,
> soothe the hearts of *N.* and *N.*,
> and grant that through the prayers of Mary,
> who grieved by the cross of her Son,
> you may enlighten their faith,
> give hope to their hearts,
> and peace to their lives.

> Lord,
> grant mercy to all the members of this family
> and comfort them with the hope
> that one day we will all live with you,
> with your Son Jesus Christ, and the Holy Spirit,
> for ever and ever.

> *R/.* Amen.

*Or:*

> Lord,
> God of all creation
> we bless and thank you for your tender care.
> Receive this life you created in love
> and comfort your faithful people in their time of loss
> with the assurance of your unfailing mercy.
>
> We ask this through Christ our Lord.
>
> *R/.* Amen.

**Concluding Rite**

*The leader concludes the rite by signing himself or herself with the sign of the cross and saying:*

> May God give us peace in our sorrow,
> consolation in our grief,
> and strength to accept his will in all things.
>
> *R/.* Amen.

# ORDER *for the* NAMING *and* COMMENDATION *of an* INFANT WHO DIED *before* BIRTH

In times of death and grief, the rites and prayers of the church do not always respond to the need of many parents to name their child and commend it in faith to the loving mercy of God, when it is not possible to celebrate the funeral liturgy or the rite of committal. The following rite is provided for use as a means of responding to these parental needs.

The *Order for the Naming and Commendation of an Infant Who Died before Birth* seeks to set the death of an infant within the context of faith, and to unite the grieving parents and family members to the merciful God, whose love was revealed to us in the death and resurrection of Jesus Christ. The rite is not intended to offer certainty to the parents, but to provide them with a celebration based on Christian faith and hope.

If the body of the infant is not present during the service, some other reminder of the child may be present during the celebration.

The term "minister" is used in this rite to refer to priests, deacons, or lay ministers. When a particular prayer is reserved to a priest or deacon, the words "priest" or "deacon" are used. The rites and prayers proper to a lay person are so indicated in the rite.

## Introductory Rites

*When all have gathered, a suitable song may be sung.*

*The minister says:*

> In the name of the Father, and of the Son, and of the Holy Spirit.

*All make the sign of the cross and reply:*

> **R/.** Amen.

*Using one of the following greetings, the minister greets those present.*

*[A] A minister who is a priest or deacon greets those present in the following or other suitable words, taken mainly from sacred Scripture.*

> May the peace and consolation of the Lord be with you.

> **R/.** And with your Spirit.

*[B] A lay minister greets those present in the following words:*

> Let us praise the God of peace and consolation. Blessed be God for ever.

> **R/.** Blessed be God for ever.

*In the following or similar words, which should always be adapted to suit the particular situation, the minister prepares the parents and others present for the celebration.*

> For those who trust in God,
> in the pain of sorrow there is consolation
> in the face of despair there is hope,
> in the midst of death there is life.
> **N.** and **N.**, as we mourn the death of your child
> we place ourselves in the hands of God
> and ask for strength, for healing and for love.

## Naming of the Child

*The minister then asks the parents to name their child.*

> What name do you give your child?

*The parents respond:* **N.**

*If the body of the infant is present, the minister may then trace the sign of the cross on or over the body of the infant, and, if appropriate, may also invite the parents and others present to do the same. The minister first says:*

> In the name of the Christian community I sign **N.** (or *this child*) with the sign of the cross [and I invite *his/her* parents (and those who are present) to do the same].

## Reading of the Word of God

*A reader, another person present, or the minister reads a text of sacred Scripture (Mark 10:13–16)*

> Brothers and sisters, listen to the words of the Gospel of Mark:
>
> People were bringing children to Jesus that he might touch them, but the disciples rebuked the people. When Jesus saw this he became indignant and said to the disciples, "Let the children come to me; do not prevent them, for the kingdom of God belongs to such as these. Amen, I say to you, who ever does not accept the kingdom of God like a child will not enter it." Then he embraced the children and blessed them, placing his hands on them.

*Or:*

Isaiah 49:8–13
> *In a time of favor I answer you, on the day of salvation*
> *I help you.*

Romans 8:18–27
> *In hope we were saved.*

Romans 8:26–31
> *If God is for us, who can be against us?*

Colossians 1:9–12
> *We have been praying for you unceasingly.*

*As circumstances suggest, the minister may give those present a brief explanation of the biblical text, so that they may understand through faith the meaning of the celebration.*

## Blessing of the Parents

*If desired, the minister may bless the parents of the infant using the following blessing taken from the* Book of Blessings: Order for the Blessing of Parents after a Miscarriage.

*The minister invites all to pray using these or similar words:*
> Let us pray to God who throughout the ages has heard
> the cries of parents.

*After a brief pause for silent prayer, a minister who is a priest or deacon says the prayer of blessing with hands outstretched over the parents; a lay minister says the prayer with hands joined.*

Compassionate God,
soothe the hearts of **N.** and **N.**,
and grant that through the prayers of Mary,
who grieved by the cross of her Son,
you may enlighten their faith,
give hope to their hearts,
and peace to their lives.

Lord,
grant mercy to all the members of this family
and comfort them with the hope
that one day we will all live with you,
with your Son Jesus Christ,
and the Holy Spirit,
for ever and ever.

**R/.** Amen.

*Or:*

Lord,
God of all creation
we bless and thank you for your tender care.
Receive this life you created in love
and comfort your people
in their time of loss
with the assurance of your unfailing mercy.
We ask this through Christ our Lord.

**R/.** Amen.

**Blessing of the Body**

*Using the following words, the minister blesses the body of the deceased child.*

> Trusting in Jesus, the loving Savior,
> who gathered children into his arms
> and blessed the little ones,
> we now commend this infant [*N.*]
> to that same embrace of love,
> in the hope that *he/she* will rejoice
> and be happy in the presence of Christ.

*Then all join the minister saying:*

> *R/.* May the angels and saints lead *him/her* to the place of light and peace where one day we will be brought together again.

*The minister continues:*

> Lord Jesus,
> lovingly receive this little child;
> bless *him/her*
> and take *him/her* to your Father.
> We ask this in hope, and we pray:
>
> Lord, have mercy.
> *R/.* Lord, have mercy.
> Christ, have mercy.
> *R/.* Christ, have mercy.
> Lord, have mercy.
> *R/.* Lord, have mercy.

## The Lord's Prayer

*Using the following or similar words, the minister invites those present to pray the Lord's Prayer.*

> When Jesus gathered his disciples around him, he taught them to pray:

> *All:* Our Father....

## Prayer of Commendation

*The minister then says the following prayer.*

> Tender Shepherd of the flock,
> **N.** now lies cradled in your love.
> Soothe the hearts of *his/her* parents
> and bring peace to their lives.
> Enlighten their faith
> and give hope to their hearts.

> Loving God,
> grant mercy to your entire family
> in this time of suffering.
> Comfort us with the hope that this child **N.**
> lives with you and your Son, Jesus Christ,
> and the Holy Spirit,
> for ever and ever.

> *R/.* Amen.

## Blessing

*Using one of the following blessings, the minister blesses those present.*

*[A] A minister who is a priest or deacon says:*

> May the God of all consolation bring you comfort and peace, in the name of the Father, and of the Son, and of the Holy Spirit.
>
> *R/.* Amen.

*[B] A lay minister invokes God's blessing and signs himself or herself with the sign of the cross, saying:*

> May the God of all consolation bring us comfort and peace, in the name of the Father, and of the Son, and of the Holy Spirit.
>
> *R/.* Amen.

*The celebration may end with a suitable song.*

---

# Liturgy *of* Remembrance

*When all have gathered, a suitable song may be sung.*

**Greeting and Opening Prayer**

*The priest invites everyone to make the sign of the cross.*

*Priest:*

> We have gathered here today to commend
> a beloved child, *N.*, to our heavenly Father,
> to assure *[parents] N.* and *N.* of God's everlasting love,
> and to acknowledge the deep sorrow in this loss.

> *N.* and *N.*, as we mourn with you
> the loss of *N.*,
> we stand with you, asking for God's strength,
> for God's healing,
> and for God's love.

> Let us pray.

> Heavenly Father,
> your Son took little children into his arms
> and blessed them.
> Grant to us now the assurance that *N.*
> is encircled by those arms of love.
> In the midst of our grief,

strengthen through the Holy Spirit
our faith and hope
in your Son,
Jesus Christ our Lord.

*R/.* Amen.

*All are seated.*

*An appropriate psalm may be sung here.*

## Scripture

*A family member or the priest stands and proclaims the Scripture (Mark 10:13–16,* New American Bible*):*

A reading from the Holy Gospel according to Mark.

People were bringing children to him that he might touch them, but the disciples rebuked them. When Jesus saw this he became indignant and said to them, "Let the children come to me; do not prevent them, for the kingdom of God belongs to such as these. Amen, I say to you, whoever does not accept the kingdom of God like a child will not enter it." Then he embraced them and blessed them, placing his hands on them.

The Gospel of the Lord.

*R/.* Praise to you, Lord Jesus Christ.

**Reflection**

*The priest or family member offers a brief reflection and/or reads an appropriate poem.*

**Intercessions**

*Priest:*

> Let us lay our prayers before the One who is resurrection and life.
>
> *R/.* Lord, hear our prayer.

*A family member reads the intercessions:*

> For *N.*, God's work of art,
> resting now gently in the arms of God.
> We pray to the Lord. *R/.*
>
> For *[parents]* *N.* and *N.*, as they mourn the loss
>   of *N.*
> For the comfort and care of family and friends.
> We pray to the Lord. *R/.*
>
> For *[mother]* *N.*,
> for healing, for strength and for abundant health.
> We pray to the Lord. *R/..*
>
> For the nurses, doctors and hospital workers who cared
>   for *N.* and who continue to care for *[mother]* *N.*
> May their hands be guided by the healing hands of Christ.
> We pray to the Lord. *R/.*

For all who have died and dwell now in God's eternal love
and peace.
We pray to the Lord. *R/.*

## The Lord's Prayer

*Priest:*

> For those who trust in God,
> in the pain of sorrow there is consolation,
> in the face of despair there is hope,
> in the midst of death there is life.
>
> Trusting in God's everlasting love, let us pray now,
> in the words our Savior gave us.
>
> *All:* Our Father…

## Closing Prayer

*Priest:*

> Let us pray.
>
> O God, we offer our thanks for *N.*,
> for the potential of *her/his* life which came to us
> as a precious gift from you,
> even though that potential
> was not realized as we would have wished.

Although we come with sorrow and with tears,
we trust in your unfailing love.
We know that nothing can separate us from your love.
We acknowledge that even though *N.* was part of our
lives for a short time, *she/he* has left a mark that will
never be lost.

We thank you too for the promise that what we see here
in this world is not all there is,
and for the hope of seeing *her/him* again because of the
death and resurrection of Jesus Christ.

Increase our capacity to trust in your grace,
even through our loss.
Despite the emptiness that we now feel,
we know that *N.* is safe in your arms of love.

O God, help and comfort *[parents]* *N.* and *N.*,
and each one who feels this loss sharply.
Continue to show your grace to this family.
And may your love light the way that leads
    to lasting peace.

We ask this through Christ, our Lord.

*R/.* Amen.

*The celebration may end with a suitable song.*

---

# PRAYER *with* SIBLINGS, COUSINS, *and* OTHER CHILDREN

*All sing together:*

## All Night, All Day

All night, all day, an-gels watch-ing o-ver me, my Lord. All night, all day, an-gels watch-ing o-ver me.

African American traditional

*Parent:*

In the Name of the Father, and of the Son, and of the Holy Spirit.

**R/.** Amen.

*Parent:*

There are angels watching over us, keeping us safe, keeping us close to God. Today we remember *N*. We didn't get to know *her/him* the way we had hoped, but *she/he* has filled up our hearts and changed our lives forever. We ask God and all the angels to be with us as we pray today.

Do not be worried or afraid! Let God know all that troubles you, and give thanks for the many blessings you have been given. God will be with us, giving us strength, and helping us always.

*(Philippians 4:6 and Isaiah 41:10 paraphrase)*

**Litany of Gratitude**

*Parent:*

We know that God hears our prayers and stays with us each day. Because we love *N.* very much, and because we love God, who put *her/him* in our lives, let's say "Thank you, God" for all the things we are grateful for.

For the sun, the moon, and all the stars in the sky:
   *R/.* Thank you, God.

For the rivers, the lakes, and the oceans and all the creatures that swim in them:
   *R/.* Thank you, God.

For all the leaves on the trees, for the soft grass that we play in:
   *R/.* Thank you, God.

For all our friends, who care for us and who play with us:
   *R/.* Thank you, God.

For all the members of our family, for those we can see and those we cannot:
   *R/.* Thank you, God.

For the angels, for *N.*, and all those in heaven who watch over us all night and all day:
   *R/.* Thank you, God.

For God who makes all things with love, no matter how big or how small:
   *R/.* Thank you, God.

What else are we thankful for?
   *(Each time, R/.* Thank you, God.*)*

Thank you, God, for this beautiful life you have given us. Keep us safe and help us to know that you are always with us.

Let us pray together the Angel of God [*or* the Lord's Prayer, *or* the Hail Mary].

*All:* Angel of God, my guardian dear,
to whom God's love commits me here,
ever this day be at my side,
to light and guard,
to rule and guide.

Amen.

*All sing once more:*

## All Night, All Day

All night, all day, an - gels watch-ing o-ver
me, my Lord. All night, all day,
an - gels watch-ing o - ver me.

African American traditional

---

# EVENING LITURGY *of the* WORD *and* RITUAL *of* LIGHT

## Gathering

*All remain seated as gathering song begins.*

*After the refrain has been sung a number of times, the priest stands and gestures for all to do the same. The refrain is sung a few more times before subsiding.*

### Confitemini Domino

Con - fi - té - mi - ni    Dó - mi - no
Llé - na - nos, Se - ñor,    de tu paz,
Come and fill our hearts    with your peace.

quó - ni - am    bo - nus,    Con - fi - té - mi - ni
Por-que só - lo e - res san - to,    Llé - na - nos, Se - ñor,
You a - lone, O Lord, are ho - ly.    Come and fill our hearts

Dó - mi - no,   Al - le - lú  -  ia!
de  tu  paz,  ¡Al - le - lu  -  ya!
with you peace,  Al - le - lu  -  ia!

*Latin translation:* Give praise to the Lord for he is good, Alleluia.

*Priest and all make the sign of the cross.*

*Priest:*

> May the Father of all mercies, the God of all consolation,
> be with you all.
>
> **R/.** And with your spirit.

*Priest:*

> For those who trust in God,
> in the pain of sorrow there is consolation,
> in the face of despair there is hope,
> in the midst of death there is life.
> As we remember today the children we've dreamed of,
> those we felt in our hearts, in our bellies,
> whose memory remain with us each and every day,
> we place ourselves in the hands of God
> and ask for strength, for healing, and for love.

*All sit for the reading (Isaiah 49:1, 15–16)*

A reading from the prophet Isaiah.

Listen to me, O coastlands, pay attention, you peoples from far away! "The Lord called me before I was born, while I was in my mother's womb he named me." Can a woman forget her nursing child, or show no compassion for the child of her womb? Even these may forget, yet I will not forget you. See, I have inscribed you on the palms of my hands; your walls are continually before me.

The word of the Lord.

*R/.* Thanks be to God.

*Cantor sings the psalm.*

## The Lord Is My Shepherd

Text: Psalm 23, *The Revised Grail Psalms*, © 2010, Conception Abbey/The Grail, admin. GIA Publications, Inc.
Music: Gary Daigle, © 2012, GIA Publications, Inc.

*Cantor intones the refrain:*

## Like a Little Child

Like a    lit-tle child    in its   moth-er's arms,    my

soul will rest in    you,   my    soul will rest in   you.

Text: David Haas
Music: David Haas
© 1993, GIA Publications, Inc.

*After all sing the refrain, the reader begins the first passage (Ephesians 1:3–5) while music underpins the reading:*

> Blessed be the God and Father of our Lord Jesus Christ, who has blessed us in Christ with every spiritual blessing in the heavenly places, just as he chose us in Christ before the foundation of the world to be holy and blameless before him in love. He destined us for adoption as his children through Jesus Christ.

*Cantor sings verse one, and all respond with the refrain.*

> *My heart is not proud, my eyes do not seek*
> *the ways from above; the things that are great.*
> *The marvels beyond are not what I need*
> *for you are my peace.*

## Like a Little Child

Like a    lit-tle child    in its    moth-er's arms,    my

soul will rest    in    you,    my    soul will rest    in    you.

Text: David Haas
Music: David Haas
© 1993, GIA Publications, Inc.

*Reader reads the second passage (1 Corinthians 15:20–23).*

> Christ has been raised from the dead, the first fruits
> of those who have died. For since death came through
> a human being, the resurrection of the dead has also
> come through a human being; for as all die in Adam,
> so all will be made alive in Christ. But each in his own
> order: Christ the first fruits, then at his coming those
> who belong to Christ.

*Cantor sings verse two, and all respond with the refrain.*

> *Quiet and still, my soul is calm*
> *in your sweet embrace, like mother and child.*
> *My hope is in you; my heart is full*
> *for you are my peace.*

## Like a Little Child

Like a lit-tle child in its moth-er's arms, my

soul will rest in you, my soul will rest in you.

Text: David Haas
Music: David Haas
© 1993, GIA Publications, Inc.

*Reader reads the third passage (1 John 3:1–2).*

> See what love the Father has given us, that we should be called children of God; and that is what we are. The reason the world does not know us is that it did not know him. Beloved, we are God's children now; what we will be has not yet been revealed. What we do know is this: when he is revealed, we will be like him, for we will see him as he is.

*Cantor sings verse three, and all respond with the refrain twice.*

> *As the deer that longs for the stream,*
> *my soul longs for your, to see your face.*
> *To you I will sing and offer my thanks*
> *for you are my peace.*

## Like a Little Child

Like a lit-tle child in its moth-er's arms, my
soul will rest in you, my soul will rest in you.

Text: David Haas
Music: David Haas
© 1993, GIA Publications, Inc.

*All stand for the Gospel Acclamation.*

## Alleluia 7

Al - le - lu - ia, al-le - lu - ia, al-le - lu - ia.
Al - le - lu - ia, al-le - lu - ia, al-le lu ia.

Music: Jacques Berthier
© 1984, Ateliers et Presses de Taizé, GIA Publications, Inc., agent.

*Priest reads the gospel reading.*

A reading from the Gospel according to Luke.

People were bringing even infants to him that he
might touch them; and when the disciples saw it, they
sternly ordered them not to do it. But Jesus called for
them and said, "Let the little children come to me,
and do not stop them; for it is to such as these that the
kingdom of God belongs. Truly I tell you, whoever
does not receive the kingdom of God as a little child
will never enter it."

The Gospel of the Lord.

**R/.** Praise to you, Lord Jesus Christ.

*All are seated for a homily, spoken reflection, or silence.**

## Ritual of Light

*After a brief silence, presider reads these or similar words.*

> As we remember the little ones we didn't get to hold, the ones who remain in our hearts and on our minds, Let us call their names aloud, as God once called us forth from the womb.
>
> As you hear the name of your child read aloud, you are welcome to come forward with your family to light a candle and place it among the photos all our loved ones who live with Jesus, who will meet us again in heaven.

*Cantor intones "Lux Aeterna" (or another appropriate piece) and all respond.*

### Lux Aeterna

Lux ae - tér - na, lux ae - tér - na

lú - ce - at e - is, Dó - mi - ne.

Text: Mass for the Dead (Latin)
Music: John L. Bell
© 2011, Wild Goose Resource Group, GIA Publications, Inc., agent

---

* See Appendix, p. 199, for the text of a homily given by Fr. Robert Oldershaw on November 11, 2018.

*Three names are read, taking time to allow families space to light a candle and place it in the sand. After the third name, all sing "Lux Aeterna" again.*

*This pattern repeats until all the names have been proclaimed.*

*After all names of children have been read, the reader invites all to recognize infertility and unnamed losses using these or similar words:*

> For all children who have not been named.
>
> For all children whose names remain unknown to us.
>
> For all children who remain as dreams in our hearts,
> for whom we wait in holy longing with God.

*As the final candles are lit, cantor sings "Lux Aeterna" in its entirety.*

*Priest:*

> Holy God,
> yours is the beauty of childhood
> and yours is the fullness of years.
> Comfort us in our sorrow,
> strengthen us with hope,
> and breathe peace into our troubled hearts.
> Assure us that the love in which we rejoiced
>     for a time
> is not lost,
> and that all our children,
>     all our hopes and dreams are with you,
> safe in your eternal love and care.

We ask this in the name of Jesus Christ,
who took little children in his arms and blessed them.
Amen.

*Book of Common Worship*, adapt.

## Intercessions

*Priest:*

Knowing that God hears us when we cry,
let us lift up the needs of the world.

*Cantor intones first time, then all repeat.*

### Grant Us Peace, Lord

Grant us peace, Lord, Grant us peace.

Grant us your peace.

Music: Tony E. Alonso
© 2001, GIA Publications, Inc.

*At the conclusion of the intercessions, the priest invites all to sing the Lord's Prayer:*

*Priest:*

Gathering all our prayers into one, let us pray with
confidence to the Father.

*All:* Our Father...

**Prayer of Blessing**

*Priest:*

Compassionate God,
soothe the hearts of those gathered here today,
and grant that through the prayers of Mary,
who grieved by the cross of her Son,
you may enlighten their faith,
give hope to their hearts,
and peace to their lives.
Lord, grant mercy to all the members of this family
and comfort them with the hope
that one day we will all live with you,
with your Son Jesus Christ, and the Holy Spirit,
forever and ever.
*R/.* Amen.

May God give us peace in our sorrow,
consolation in our grief,
and strength to accept God's will in all things.
*Book of Blessings*, adapt.

Let us offer to one another a sign of Christ's peace as we
end our prayer and take leave of each other this night.

# Appendix

# Homily

## Fr. Robert Oldershaw

*Margaret, are you grieving*
*Over Goldengrove unleaving?*
*Leaves, like the things of man, you*
*With your fresh thoughts care for, can you?*
*Ah! as the heart grows older*
*It will come to such sights colder*
*By and by, nor spare a sigh*
*Though worlds of wanwood leafmeal lie;*
*And yet you will weep and know why.*
*Now no matter, child, the name:*
*Sorrow's springs are the same.*
*Nor mouth had, no nor mind, expressed*
*What heart heard of, ghost guessed:*
*It is the blight man was born for,*
*It is Margaret you mourn for.*

Gerard Manley Hopkins, 1844–1889

Wandering through the Goldengrove in recent chill days,
I've thought of little Margaret to whom the poet speaks these
tender words, and all the Margarets within us and among us,
who grieve the loss of leaves or loved ones,
barely known but warmly loved,
who have fallen much too quickly from our lives.
The goldengrove has too soon become a bare ruined choir
where once the sweet birds sang a tune,
perhaps that you alone could hear
in your longing and hoping,

desiring and despairing,
seeking and sorrowing.
*Ah! as the heart grows older*
*It will come to such* thoughts *colder…*
only if we forget the fresh thoughts, the memories, the sacred
words…

> I will never forget you.
> I who called you before you were born.
> Will I not have compassion on the child of your womb?
> I have destined you for adoption as my child through
> Jesus.
> I live who once was dead.
> I have knit you together, not only in your mother's womb,
> but long before that, in my heart.
> I have written your name on my hand…your name, the
> name I have given you, before you were dreamed of,
> thought of, hoped for.
> I will never forget.
> You are mine.


Yet, Margaret, *you will* grieve *and know why.*
*Now no matter, child, the name:*
*Sorrow's springs are the same.*


So we remember,
we must remember,
God the Father of our Lord Jesus Christ
who chose us, each and all,
all who were wished for, longed for, yearned for, prayed for.
The name is different but the spring is the same
and from the spring comes not only sorrow
but hope, not only tears but laughter.
Not only death but life.

# Appendix

And so,

we remember,
we must remember,
the God who does not take
but the God who catches,
the God who does not break hearts
but the God who mends and heals,
the God who does not demand
but the God who invites and welcomes;
let the little ones come to me,
little ones whose lives passed like
leaves in the autumn winds,
little ones who never saw the light,
little ones who remain a mother's dream.

*Dejen que los niños vengan a mi...*

Dear God, in this month of Novembering,
envelop us in the memories and hopes of the saints
whose images surround us.
And not only their memories but their hopes, and ours,
of what is yet to be.

The Day of the Lord,
when the Lord God will drop his august dignity
like a worn-out coat,
will hop and clap with the once-lame,
sing barbershop with the once-mute,
join hands in a round dance with happy mothers
and their tiny ones and dream children—
those living in our hearts and in our hopes,
and those alive in you alone...

all…
everyone…
one vast, joyful communion,
singing, shouting, dancing, and leaping forever and ever.

Amen.

# APPENDIX

A RECORDING OF THE FOLLOWING SONG
SUGGESTIONS IS AVAILABLE (CD-1061),
AS WELL AS THE PRINTED MUSIC COLLECTION FOR
*OF WOMB AND TOMB* (G-9817).

| | | |
|---|---|---|
| And Jesus Said | Tony Alonso | G-7075 |
| The Lord Is My Shepherd | Gary Daigle | G-8283 |
| Do Not Be Afraid | Jeanne Cotter | G-9325 |
| God Is Always There | Michael Mahler | G-6044 |
| The Clouds' Veil | Liam Lawton, arr. John McCann | G-4664 |
| Be Still and Know | John L. Bell | G-4382 |
| Turn My Heart, O God | Marty Haugen | G-5864 |
| Pieta: The Silence and the Sorrow | Liam Lawton, arr. John McCann | G-5291 |
| Come to Me, O Weary Traveler | Paul Tate | G-9135 |
| In the Arms of God | Tony Alonso | G-7585 |
| In the Morning, in the Evening | Bex Gaunt | G-9873 |
| All Is Holy | Jeanne Cotter | G-9324 |
| Like a Little Child | David Haas | G-3956 |
| Quietly, Peacefully | Lori True | G-6718 |
| Love, Burn Bright | Chris de Silva | G-8714 |
| Lux Aeterna | John L. Bell | G-8017 |

# BOOK *of* REMEMBRANCE

**MAY THE ANGELS LEAD YOU INTO PARADISE;
MAY THE MARTYRS COME TO WELCOME YOU
AND TAKE YOU TO THE HOLY CITY,
THE NEW AND ETERNAL JERUSALEM.**

Baby Rupp

Kelley Lynn Williams

Francis Gordon Gómez

Terese Kennedy-Farrell

Gabriel Thomas Kennedy-Farrell

Julian Elizabeth Kennedy-Farrell

Aine Kennedy-Farrell

Bridgid Kennedy-Farrell

Daniel Joseph Kennedy-Farrell

February Baby Callam

November Baby Callam

Francis Reynolds

Sarah Reynolds

Lulu Reynolds

_____

_____

_____

_____

_____